Green Finance and Investment



# Enabling Conditions for Bioenergy Finance and Investment in Colombia

OECD

BETTER POLICIES FOR BETTER LIVES

**Please cite this publication as:**
OECD (2022), *Enabling Conditions for Bioenergy Finance and Investment in Colombia*, Green Finance and Investment, OECD Publishing, Paris, https://doi.org/10.1787/20f760d6-en.

ISBN 978-92-64-80452-4 (print)
ISBN 978-92-64-46390-5 (pdf)
ISBN 978-92-64-58941-4 (HTML)
ISBN 978-92-64-95485-4 (epub)

Green Finance and Investment
ISSN 2409-0336 (print)
ISSN 2409-0344 (online)

**Photo credits:** Cover © Jess Kraft/Shutterstock.com.

Corrigenda to publications may be found on line at: www.oecd.org/about/publishing/corrigenda.htm.

# Preface

Colombia has taken a leading role on climate action in Latin America and the Caribbean, committing to reduce emissions relative to 2014 by 51% by 2030. The government has equally pushed forward its environment and climate agendas with measures such as the 2018 Green Growth Policy, the 2019 Circular Economy Strategy and the Energy Transition Law of 2021.

Renewable energy can and will play a vital role in meeting Colombia's green economy goals. The country is fortunate to have abundant renewables potential that can increase access to affordable and reliable energy benefiting all citizens while also diversifying the country's power mix to improve energy security. Renewable energy can likewise compliment Colombia's impressive hydropower capacity, which is increasingly being affected by the growing impacts of climate change.

Renewable energy projects like solar and wind developments have already attracted notable interest from investors since the country's first renewable electricity auctions in 2019. Bioenergy stands out as a strategic opportunity, tapping into residues and waste from agricultural, industrial and municipal activities. Bioenergy solutions can equally support the delivery of other policy objectives, such as reducing the amount of waste going to Colombia's landfills and increasing overall productivity of the country's agroindustry.

This report supports efforts to achieve the country's clean energy ambitions through measures that can strengthen opportunities for bioenergy development. The report assesses the current policy environment for bioenergy projects, highlighting market barriers and identifying solutions that can help to scale up finance and investment in these opportunities. The report also contains five case studies on experiences in other countries that can serve as examples and lessons learned for similar progress in Colombia.

The work taken to produce this publication is the result of the close engagement between the OECD and the Government of Colombia. I am confident that this collaborative effort will help to implement domestic policies that mobilise finance and investment in bioenergy projects in Colombia. I also hope this report serves as a starting point for dialogues with other countries in Latin America and the Caribbean to share experiences and good practices on ways to unlock finance and investment for clean energy solutions like bioenergy.

Mathias Cormann
Secretary-General, OECD

# Foreword

*Enabling conditions for bioenergy finance and investment in Colombia* is an output of the collaborative partnership between the Government of Colombia and the OECD Clean Energy Finance and Investment Mobilisation (CEFIM) programme. The CEFIM Programme aims to support governments in emerging economies to unlock finance and investment in renewable electricity and energy efficiency ("clean energy").

The OECD would like to thank the Government of Colombia for its co-operation in providing information for this report. Particular thanks are due to the Ministry of Mines and Energy, which is the CEFIM focal point in Colombia and which provided invaluable inputs and feedback to this report. CEFIM would equally like to thank contributors to the five case studies in this report, including: Jorge Casas from Manuelita, Colombia; Daniel Alves de Mattos of the Brazilian Association of Portland Cement (Associação Brasileira de Cimento Portland, ABCP); Gonzalo Visedo of the Brazilian National Syndicate of the Cement Industry (Sindicato Nacional da Indústria do Cimento, SNIC); Sezin Hizli of ENERGOM, Turkey; Oliver Luedtke of Verbio, Germany; and Gerardo Canales Gonzalez of Implementasur, Chile.

Lylah Davies and John Dulac from the OECD Environment Directorate led this project and were the main authors of this report. Cecilia Tam, Team Leader of the CEFIM Programme, oversaw the project. Dominique Haleva provided administrative support and copy-editing. This report is an output of the OECD Environment Policy Committee and its Working Party on Climate Investment and Development. The report was carried out under the overall responsibility of Walid Oueslati, Acting Head of the Environment Transitions and Resilience Division.

This project benefited from in-country support, notably through Maria Carolina Garzon Sanchez, Adviser for International Affairs of Colombia's Ministry of Mines and Energy, who co-ordinated review and comments from various departments within the Government of Colombia. The report was reviewed and received feedback from Jorge Carbonell of the OECD Secretariat and Alejandro Hernandez, Paolo Frankl and Jeremy Moorhouse of the International Energy Agency. Various experts provided review, including: Ruben Contreras of the United Nations Economic Commission for Latin America and the Caribbean (CEPAL); Catalina Cano Zapata and Santiago Abraham Montoya Tamayo of Bancolombia; Yineth Piñeros of the Jorge Tadeo Lozano University (Universidad Jorge Tadeo Lozano); Jose Maria Rincon of the National University of Colombia (Universidad Nacional de Colombia); and Angela Cadena of the Los Andes University (Universidad de los Andes).

This report was made possible thanks to generous funding from Denmark.

# Table of contents

## Tables

## Figures



## Boxes

# Abbreviations and acronyms

| | |
|---|---|
| ABCP | Brazilian Portland Cement Association (Associação Brasileira de Cimento Portland) |
| Asocaña | Colombian Sugarcane Growers Association (Asociación de Cultivadores de Caña de Azúcar) |
| AUD | Australian Dollar |
| CBG | compressed biogas |
| CICC | Intersectoral Commission on Climate Change (Comisión Intersectorial de Cambio Climático) |
| CNG | compressed natural gas |
| $CO_2$ | carbon dioxide |
| CONAMA | National Council for the Environment (Conselho Nacional do Meio Ambiente), Brazil |
| CONPES | National Council for Social and Economic Policy (Consejo Nacional de Política Económica y Social) |
| CREG | Energy and Gas Regulation Commission (Comisión de Regulación de Energía y Gas) |
| DNP | National Planning Department (Departamento Nacional de Planeación) |
| EIT | European Institute of Innovation and Technology |
| ENRO | National Organic Waste Strategy (Estrategia Nacional de Residuos Orgánicos), Chile |
| EUR | Euro |
| FDI | foreign direct investment |
| FENOGE | Fund for Non-conventional Energy and Efficient Energy Management (Fondo de Energías No Convencionales y Gestión Eficiente de la Energía) |
| Findeter | Territorial Development Finance (Financiera De Desarrollo Territorial) |
| g | grammes |
| GDP | gross dometic product |
| GHG | greenhouse gas emission |
| GW | gigawatt |
| GWh | gigawatt-hour |
| IDCOL | Infrastructure Development Company Limited (Bangladesh) |
| INR | Indian Rupee |
| IPSE | Institute of Planning and Promotion of Energy Solutions in Non-Interconnected Zones (Instituto de Planificación y Promoción de Soluciones Energéticas para Zonas No Interconectadas) |
| kWh | kilowatt-hours |
| LNG | liquefied natural gas |
| $m^2$ | square metre |
| MADS | Ministry of Environment and Sustainable Development (Ministerio de Ambiente y Desarrollo Sostenible) |
| MENR | Ministry of Energy and Natural Resources (Turkey) |
| MJ | megajoule |
| MME | Ministry of Mines and Energy (Ministerio de Minas y Energía) |
| MNRE | Ministry of New and Renewable Energy, India |
| MSW | municipal solid waste |
| Mtoe | million tonnes of oil equivalent |
| MW | megawatt |
| MWh | megawatt-hour |
| MRV | measurement, reporting and verification |
| NAMA | Nationally Appropriate Mitigation Action |
| NCRE | non-conventional renewable energy |
| NDC | Nationally Determined Contribution |
| PEN | National Energy Plan (Plan Energético Nacional) |
| PNRS | Brazilian National Policy of Solid Waste (Política Nacional de Resíduos Sólidos) |
| PPA | power purchase agreement |
| PPP | public-private partnership |

| | |
|---|---|
| PROURE | Programme for the Rational and Efficient Use of Energy and other NCRE (non-conventional renewable energy) |
| PV | photovoltaic |
| REAP | Renewable Energy Action Plan (Turkey) |
| REC | renewable energy certificate |
| RDF | refuse-derived fuel |
| RERED | Rural Electrification and Renewable Energy Development |
| SDG | Sustainable Development Goals |
| SISCLIMA | National System for Climate Change (Sistema Nacional de Cambio Climático) |
| SNIC | National Union of Cement Industry (Sindicato Nacional da Indústria do Cimento), Brazil |
| TWh | terawatt-hours |
| UPME | Planning Unit of the Ministry of Mines and Energy (Unidad de Planeación Minero Energética) |
| USD | United States dollar |
| YEKDEM | Renewable Energy Support Mechanism (Yenilenebilir Enerji Kaynakları Destekleme Mekanizması) |
| ZNI | non-interconnected zones (zonas no interconectadas) |

# Executive summary

Colombia is a country abundant in energy resources, including not only fossil fuels but also important hydro capacity and substantial renewable energy potential. Yet, declining oil and natural gas reserves, alongside the growing intensity of "El Niño" events and other climate change impacts on hydropower installations, have placed increasing strains on the country's capacity to ensure secure, reliable and affordable energy. Commitment to climate action, including the government's revised Nationally Determined Contribution (NDC) under the Paris Agreement, equally calls for measures to unlock the clean energy transition in Colombia in order to achieve substantial reductions in the country's greenhouse gas (GHG) emissions.

***Strategic policies have established the imperative for clean energy development***

To realise its clean energy ambitions and enable the necessary mobilisation of finance and investment for these solutions, the government has set forth a number of important policy strategies, including the 2018 Green Growth Policy, the 2019 National Circular Economy Strategy and a forthcoming 2021 Energy Transition Policy. These high-level policies all note the role clean energy solutions like sustainable bioenergy can play in supporting decarbonisation objectives, whilst also achieving a number of other socioeconomic ambitions, including improved reliability of energy supply, reduced dependence on energy imports and improved access to affordable and reliable energy in areas that are not connected to the national electricity grid.

***Bioenergy solutions can play a key role in achieving the country's clean energy ambitions***

Bioenergy can play a strategic role in meeting multiple policy objectives, given the opportunities to use residues and waste from agricultural, industrial and municipal activities for clean energy production. Developments to date have been concentrated on biofuels for transport and to a lesser extent bagasse use for electricity and heat co-generation in the sugar and palm industries, but there remains considerable, unexploited potential to use other agricultural residues and waste streams from industrial and municipal activities, with potential added environmental benefits from reduced amounts of waste going to the country's aging and capacity-limited landfills. Unlocking these opportunities requires further policy actions to encourage clean energy generation from waste and residues, particularly as these projects can be more difficult in nature given the complex chain of sourcing, sorting and treatment of waste. Support for innovation and local technical capacity can also help to enable solutions fit for the Colombian context.

***Clearer targets in energy planning will signal the prospects for bioenergy development***

Strategic action is needed if Colombia is to unlock its considerable bioenergy resource potential, where expanding opportunities for these solutions requires a more in-depth vision on the role bioenergy technologies can play in the country's energy transition over the next decade and beyond. Recent developments such as the country's first renewable energy auctions in 2019 highlighted the clear interest from both domestic and international actors in engaging in Colombia's clean energy market. Yet, opening the door for scaled-up finance and investment in bioenergy additions, particularly in face of falling solar and wind prices, will require more targeted measures to see similar levels of engagement from project developers and investors.

Notably, opportunities for bioenergy projects need to be reflected more clearly in energy market policy, regulations and electricity market design. For example, current electricity expansion plans do not adequately reflect national policy priorities such as the 2020 Bioeconomy Strategy, and reliance on the pipeline of planned capacity additions for the development of these plans does not account for the techno-economic potential of bioenergy solutions in meeting the government's strategic policy ambitions. Current plans also do not highlight the role bioenergy can play, for instance through dispatchable and round-the-clock power, in supporting further deployment of variable renewable electricity sources.

***Early bioenergy developments highlight the importance of coherent regulatory guidance***

Rules and regulations around electricity market access in an extensively integrated market, which compels high dependence on retailer willingness to connect distributed generation projects, make for critical barriers to bioenergy capacity additions. Useful lessons can be extracted from experiences over the last two decades with sugarcane and palm oil co-generation, which greatly benefited from regulatory reforms and market incentives. These measures enabled a clearer business model for those industries, resulting in a nearly six-fold increase in electricity sales from grid connected co-generation between 2000 and 2017.

Colombia's strong framework for waste collection and disposal can be strengthened to encourage greater sorting, treatment, recycling and re-use of waste streams, building upon recommendations from the country's accession to the OECD. Lack of incentives in the current regulatory environment add to challenges for bioenergy development, as landfill fees are low and the existing framework does not encourage alternative pathways for waste treatment, in spite of calls to reduce waste disposal. The number of actors, authorities and regulations influencing waste-to-energy also makes it challenging to navigate development of such applications.

***Better access to affordable finance will help to lower the cost of bioenergy projects***

Green finance flows continue to grow in Colombia, thanks to on-going capital market reforms and the government's emerging sustainable finance framework. Yet, access to finance is a critical barrier for many bioenergy projects, especially for smaller players, who in addition to limited experience with bioenergy technologies also often lack sufficient credit history to get a project loan. Lender unfamiliarity with these types of projects and overall perceptions of risk by financial actors also mean the cost of finance is typically high, even for more established actors such as sugarcane co-generators, who can still rely on corporate credit lines to finance capacity additions. Targeted support, such as microfinance arrangements with local financial institutions, and use of de-risking mechanisms to address project risks will enable better financing conditions for projects and increase the attractiveness of bioenergy solutions in the market.

## Actions to unlock the opportunity for sustainable bioenergy development

The government of Colombia can take a number of actions to improve the enabling environment for bioenergy finance and investment, building upon measures that supported bioenergy developments in the sugar and palm industries as well as by drawing insights and lessons learned from other country experiences, such as the bioenergy projects highlighted under the case studies in the Annex of this report.

Recommended actions include establishing clear targets for bioenergy capacity additions in energy and electricity market plans, whilst improving institutional co-ordination to ensure the opportunities for bioenergy development are clearly reflected across related public and economic policies. Strengthening market signals such as progressive increases in landfill fees paid by waste producers, which remain low compared to other OECD countries, will also improve the economics of sorting, treatment and recovery of waste for energy production, providing the needed incentive for businesses and industry to seek alternative pathways to waste disposal.

Regulatory measures building upon past reforms liberalising the electricity market should also address the influence of incumbents and seek to increase overall fairness and non-discriminatory access to the grid, as current rules may limit opportunities for some renewable energy technologies. For example, addressing limitations in bilateral agreements, especially for smaller generation sizes, and providing clearer guidance on power wheeling arrangements will help facilitate businesses offering and seeking clean electricity generation. The government should also review its renewable energy portfolio standards, which do not provide retailers with sufficient incentive to work with self-generators, co-generators and unregulated consumers that could increase overall bioenergy capacity in the market.

The government can also work with financial stakeholders, building upon existing funds such as "Findeter" financing for local and municipal infrastructure projects, to assess opportunities to implement targeted financial measures that increase the flows of capital to bioenergy projects. This can include use of de-risking tools such as guarantees and concessional credit to encourage improved access to finance and to address risks in lending to bioenergy projects. The government can also pursue opportunities for blended finance with development funds and climate finance to target public support in a way that catalyses private capital for bioenergy projects.

Lastly, training and capacity building, alongside public support for new and innovative technologies and business models, can help to develop a robust pipeline of bioenergy solutions adapted to the Colombian context. Working with domestic stakeholders like Colombia's National Centre for Cleaner Production and Environmental Technology can build awareness in the market and enable technical capacity to implement bioenergy projects, whilst improving resource efficiency and circular economy across important economic sectors like industry and agriculture. Engagement of stakeholders will equally help to identify opportunities for policy actions and market incentives that reduce barriers to bioenergy development and encourage active participation of private capital in these projects.

# 1 Energy sector trends and clean energy prospects

Colombia relies heavily on fossil fuels to meet its energy needs, but declining domestic reserves for oil and gas are contributing to growing dependence on energy imports. This is evidenced by increased reliance on fossil fuel inputs for power generation, despite the country's significant hydropower installations. Droughts and constraints on water resources have also highlighted the need to diversify Colombia's power mix, and the first renewable energy auctions in 2019 and 2021 drew attention to the country's sizeable solar and wind resources. Bioenergy opportunities, by contrast, remain largely untapped, in spite of considerable available feedstock. Targeted policy interventions are needed to meet political ambitions to unlock this potential, which will also provide other benefits such as reduced waste to landfills, emissions mitigation and ability to supply local, reliable electricity.

## Introduction

Colombia has made considerable socioeconomic progress over the last two decades and is the fourth largest economy in Latin America. Gross domestic product (GDP) per capita grew ten-fold since 1990, supported in particular by exports of natural resources such as coal, crude petroleum, gems, precious metals, iron ore (including exports of manufactured steel) and agricultural products like sugar, coffee and fruits (WITS, 2021[1]). Progress on trade agreements, infrastructure developments such as Colombia's high-draught ports, and policy reforms enabling a strong legal regime for businesses also have contributed to economic growth, as has the country's geographic advantage as a gateway to and from Central America. These factors, amongst others, have all made Colombia an attractive investment destination (ITA, 2021[2]).

Foreign direct investment (FDI) as a share of GDP doubled to 4.4% between 2010 and 2019, representing over USD 14 billion that year (World Bank, 2021[3]). This has largely gone to extractive industries (i.e. fossil fuels and mining), although FDI in financial services, communication technologies and clean energy has grown substantially since the mid-2010s. For example, FDI in renewable energy development grew eight-fold between 2018 and 2021, from seven projects worth USD 446 million in 2018 to 24 projects worth USD 3.8 billion in 2020 (EFE, 2021[4]). This growth was supported , in part, by efforts by the government to promote Colombia's considerable renewable energy potential, for instance through the state promotion agency, ProColombia. In particular, the government has aimed to attract private investment, for example through tax incentives and financial guarantees, to clean energy projects that strengthen the national energy mix and that improve overall supply reliability (Procolombia, 2021[5]).

These efforts are part of strategic plans to diversify Colombia's current power sector, which is highly dependent on hydro resources that are a structural weakness during periods of drought. Regulatory and market measures in recent years have consequently aimed to increase the installed capacity of other renewable energy sources, such as Colombia's large solar and wind potential. Bioenergy is another abundant potential resource, although market development remains relatively limited.

Increased investment in Colombia's vast renewable energy resources will help to improve the reliability of domestic energy supply through low-carbon power, while equally reducing growing dependence on energy imports such as liquefied natural gas (LNG). Renewable energy deployment will equally play a central role in meeting the government's ambitious emissions reduction targets to 2030 and beyond. Still, to achieve the country's clean energy goals, additional actions are required to strengthen market conditions and scale-up investment in those renewable energy solutions.

In particular, strategic action is needed if Colombia is to unlock its substantial bioenergy potential, including largely untapped opportunities for agricultural, industrial and municipal waste applications. This paper accordingly considers the status of bioenergy and waste-to-energy solutions in Colombia, and it looks at measures the government can take to increase the flow of finance and investment to those opportunities.

## Highlights

- Fossil fuels dominate energy supply and demand in Colombia, with increasing implications for energy security and affordability as imports grow in order to compensate declining reserves of oil and natural gas. By 2050, fossil fuel imports could reach nearly 70% of total energy supply if measures are not taken to address the country's growing dependence.
- Abundant water resources have played a central role in developing Colombia's low-cost power system, but extreme weather events and the increasing impacts of climate change are amplifying the need to diversify the power system.
- Colombia has impressive renewable energy potential, including large, untapped solar, wind and bioenergy resources. Investment in these clean energy solutions can help to increase reliability and affordability of energy supply whilst equally decarbonising the country's energy mix.
- Wind and solar capacity additions have seen impressive growth in recent years, thanks to the introduction of renewable energy auctions. Bioenergy production, however, remains limited to biofuel production and some electricity and heat cogeneration in the sugar and palm industries.
- This gap is due in part to higher investment needs for bioenergy technologies, such as anaerobic digestion and gasification plants, but capital costs do not capture the socio-economic benefits from those projects, such as the value of reduced waste to landfills, emissions mitigation and the ability to supply local, reliable electricity.
- Examples such as the Doña Juana biogas facility in Bogotá illustrate the opportunity to produce clean energy using waste and residues from agricultural, industrial and municipal activities. Experiences and lessons learned from bioenergy developments in other countries, including those highlighted throughout this report, also highlight measures that Colombia can take to kick-start bioenergy projects.

Economic progress and population growth have contributed to steadily rising energy consumption in Colombia since the early 2000s, including a sharp increase in electricity demand, in spite of overall energy intensity improvements (in terms of units of energy consumed per unit of GDP). Industry and buildings in particular experienced big shifts to electricity over the last two decades, playing an important role in the near-doubling of electricity production between 2000 and 2018 (IEA, 2021[6]).

To meet rising demand, installed hydropower capacity was increased by around 40% since 2000, although these additions were not enough to keep up with growing generation needs, particularly in the warm phase of the El Niño–Southern Oscillation that led to important water shortages in 2015 and 2016. As a result, thermal power generation using fossil fuels swelled, reaching nearly 30% of Colombia's electricity output in the 2015-16 period (IEA, 2021[6]). When combined with oil demand in the rapidly growing transport sector, the net effect was a considerable jump in overall fossil fuel use in the mid-2010s (Figure 1.1). This came down slightly by 2018 as the effects of El Niño diminished, but fossil fuels nevertheless continue to play a major role in the country's overall energy mix.

Figure 1.1. Primary energy supply by fuel, 2000-18

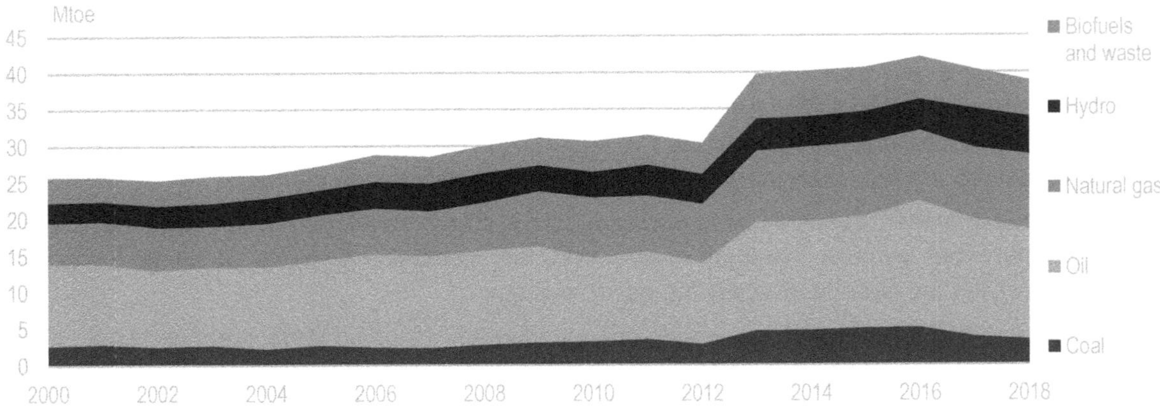


Note: Mtoe = million tonnes of oil equivalent.
Source: (IEA, 2021[6]), World Energy Balances (database).

StatLink https://stat.link/1fxc8q

## Colombia is rich in natural resources, with large untapped renewable energy potential

Colombia boasts extensive energy resources with abundant hydro as well as sizeable reserves of coal, oil and natural gas. The country's fossil fuel reserves have been exploited for both consumption and export, providing low-cost energy domestically whilst supporting overall economic growth. Notably, Colombia has considerable coal reserves and was the world's 12th largest coal producer in 2019, making it the largest in Latin America with more than ten times the coal production of the second largest producer in the region, Mexico (EIA, 2020[7]). Exploitation is directed primarily at exports and, in 2019, Colombia shipped the equivalent of more than 47 Mtoe, making it the world's sixth largest coal exporter, with important economic implications (around 0.6% of national GDP in 2019) from coal rents (World Bank, 2021[8]).

Colombia also depends heavily on its oil reserves, both for domestic consumption and for export, where the country ranked as the sixth largest crude oil exporter to the United States in 2017 (EIA, 2020[7]). Colombia produced about 918 thousand barrels per day of petroleum oil and other related liquids in 2019, equal to 45 Mtoe in annual supply, thus making it the third largest oil producer in Latin America after Brazil and Venezuela. Yet, reserves are declining, and energy imports are increasing, thereby undermining national energy security. With proven reserves standing at around two billion barrels (about 275 Mtoe), there only remain roughly six years of current levels of domestic production. In addition, output is declining, and lower global oil prices have caused exploration activities to dwindle (Reuters, 2021[9]).

Natural gas reserves are also in decline and are relatively modest by regional standards. Around 95 Mtoe remained at the end of 2020, whereby in comparison, Mexico and Argentina had about 160 Mtoe and 325 Mtoe, respectively (EIA, 2020[7]). Outstanding reserves in Colombia only equate to around eight years of domestic consumption (Reuters, 2021[9]), and the country became a net importer in 2016 (EIA, 2020[7]). The Planning Unit of the Ministry of Mines and Energy (Unidad de Planeación Minero Energética, UPME) consequently recommended adding two new LNG re-gasification plants along the Pacific Coast to ensure supply for power generation to central and southern Colombia (Kraul, 2020[10]). These have not yet been constructed, though they would have long-term implications for continued reliance on imported natural gas.

Colombia has equally been fortunate to have been one of the most water-rich countries in the world (FAO, 2003[11]), with historically abundant water resources that allowed the country to develop a low-cost power system, which boasts the third largest installed hydropower capacity in South America at nearly

12 gigawatts (GW) (IHA, 2020[12]). Yet, water availability has declined in the last decade, due to the impacts of climate change and increasing demand from population and economic growth. The country has also experienced extreme weather events linked to El Niño and La Niña phenomena, which respectively can cause prolonged droughts and extreme flooding, thereby impacting hydro electricity production. Recent El Niño events have had a particularly severe impact on hydropower reserves, amplifying the need to diversify the power system.

In response, the government has sought to exploit greater use of other renewable energy sources, which likewise have considerable potential (Figure 1.2). In particular, Colombia has favourable conditions for wind and solar energy, which have remained mostly untapped (Norton Rose Fulbright, 2016[13]). For example, wind potential in the department of La Guajira in the north of Colombia is estimated at 18 GW (Mordor Intelligence, 2020[14]), more than all currently installed electricity generation capacity in Colombia. Average annual wind speeds in certain locations off-shore of La Guajira are as high as 11 metres per second (IDEAM, 2020[15]), making Colombia one of only two regions in all of Latin America to reach these high levels, at more than double the minimum wind speed needed for utility-scale installations (Norton Rose Fulbright, 2016[13]).

Colombia also has strong solar potential, with the country averaging 4.5 kilowatt-hours (kWh) per square metre ($m^2$) per day (UPME, 2015[16]), where the higher bracket for high solar potential is benchmarked at 3.7 kWh/$m^2$ (Vesga, 2021[17]). By comparison, Spain, which had over 11 GW of installed solar capacity in 2019, receives on average around 3-3.5 kWh/$m^2$ per day in solar irradiance, while in Germany, with over 49 GW of installed solar capacity in 2019, this number averages around 2.2-3.2 kWh/$m^2$ per day (World Bank, 2020[18]); (IRENA, 2020[19]). Potential for large-scale solar generation is therefore particularly strong in Colombia, especially in the Orinoco region in the east and San Andrés islands in the Caribbean, where average radiation reaches as high as 6.0 kWh/$m^2$ per day (IDEAM, 2020[20]); (López et al., 2020[21]).

**Figure 1.2. Renewable electricity potential and utilisation rate in Colombia, 2019**

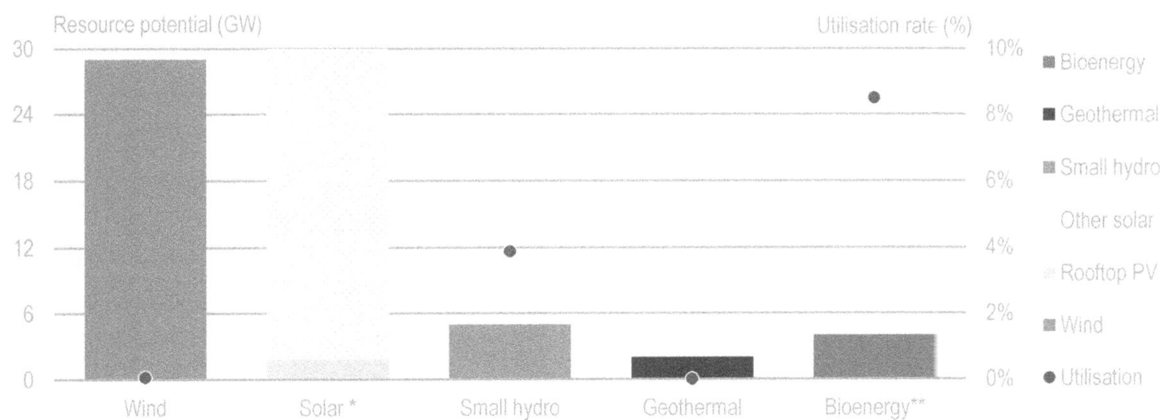


Notes: PV = photovoltaic. Solar * potential includes specific estimates for rooftop PV installations in large cities (solid), while other solar (dotted) potential is purely illustrative, given average solar radiation in Colombia in comparison with Germany (roughly one-third the land size and with lower solar irradiance), which had nearly 36 GW of solar PV installed in 2013 when PV prices were considerably higher (REN21, 2014[22]). Bioenergy** only includes estimates for electricity generation capacity from agricultural residues (Benavides and Cadena, 2018[23]).
Sources: adapted from (UPME, 2015[16]); (Benavides and Cadena, 2018[23]); (IRENA, 2020[19]).

StatLink https://stat.link/t7d15x

While solar and wind potential are substantial, integrating increased levels of these variable renewable energy will require investment to open grid capacity and to improve system flexibility (e.g. using energy storage and demand-side response). In addition, wind potential is largely concentrated in regions that can be far from demand centres and thus requires investment in transmission capacity to connect supply and demand. A particular risk is that long lead times or mismatches between transmission capacity and renewable energy additions will hamper future clean energy progress. In response, the government started awarding contracts for new transmission lines in 2018 to connect a first wave of clean energy projects in La Guajira. Grid reinforcements under the government's "Caribe 5" plan[1] also aim to strengthen capacity through as much as USD 4 billion of investment in transmission and network projects in the country's Caribbean region.

Bioenergy solutions can equally contribute to a flexible clean energy system, and Colombia is fortunate to have substantial potential bioenergy feedstocks. This includes agricultural residues from palm oil and sugar crops, which are already used for the production, domestic use and export of biodiesel and bioethanol. Other residues and waste from agricultural, municipal and industrial activities remain largely untapped opportunities for bioenergy production, and these resources, often in proximity to demand centres, could be used to create a number of clean energy products for uses such as local baseload power to municipal and regional electricity networks (Figure 1.3). Bioenergy production from available domestic feedstocks would help to reduce reliance on fossil fuels and growing dependence on LNG imports. Redirecting waste streams towards energy recovery can likewise have added environmental benefits, for instance by limiting the amount of waste going to landfills or being disposed of illegally, and proper management of these available waste streams can help to ensure that clean energy production does not encourage indirect land use change impacts, such as deforestation for biofuel feedstocks.

Figure 1.3. Potential products and uses of bioenergy resources

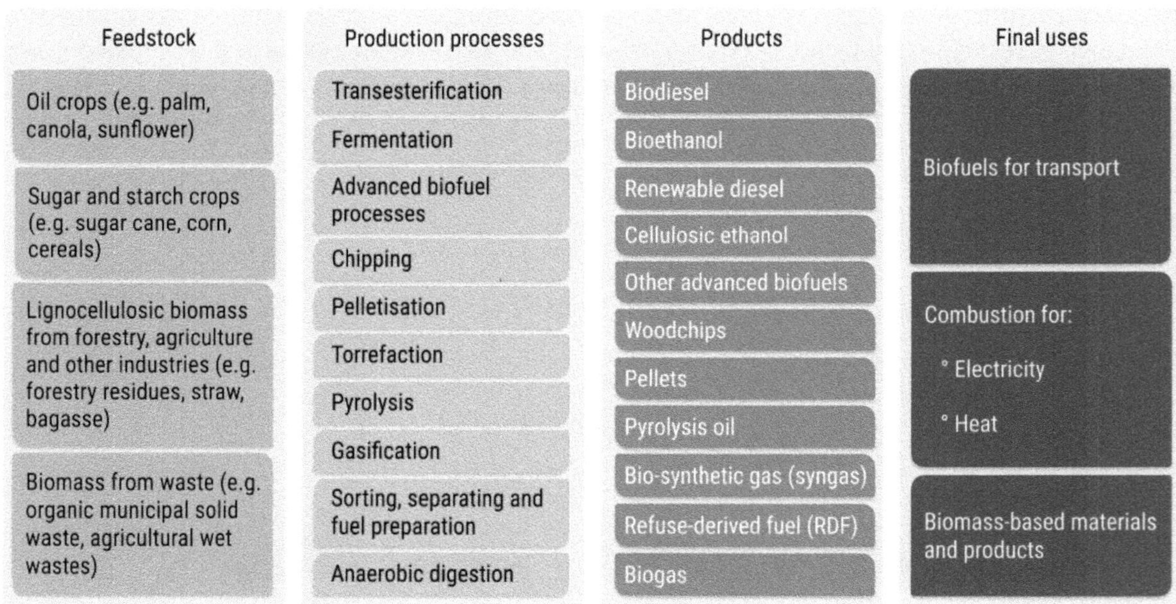


Source: adapted from (IEA, 2017[24]) Technology Roadmap: Delivering Sustainable Bioenergy.

### *Residues and waste can play a supporting role in clean energy development.*

On average, around 178 million tonnes of organic waste are produced each year in Colombia from agricultural activities (41%), livestock (59%) and the residential sector (<1%). While some of these go through a compositing process to increase their value as fertiliser, the majority is re-integrated into crops in a non-technical way, which has been linked with decreasing productivity of land (Government of Colombia, 2019[25]). Development of bioenergy solutions can thus help to improve the overall bioeconomy in Colombia, for example using biodigestion to convert organic waste from farms into bioenergy and biofertilisers.

UPME estimates that agricultural biomass residues, via direct combustion and/or anaerobic digestion, could be converted to around 8 Mtoe of energy, equivalent to roughly a fifth of Colombia's total energy supply in 2018 (UPME, 2011[26]). Residues from livestock (e.g. cattle, swine and chicken manure) could likewise generate as much as 33 terawatt-hours (TWh) of electricity, or nearly half the power supplied (77 TWh) in Colombia in 2019 (IEA, 2021[6]). A further UPME study from 2017 highlighted opportunity for biogas production, noting a technical potential of 11 TWh from agricultural residues and an additional 1.7 TWh from livestock waste (Table 1.1) (UPME, 2017[27]). For instance, biogas could be produced from bagasse residues that remain from liquid biofuel production, of which Colombia already is amongst leading global producers and is in the top ten employers in that field (IRENA, 2020[28]).

Energy generation from municipal and industrial waste also has good potential, particularly as most of this waste ends up in landfills and consequently is a significant contributor to greenhouse gas emissions (GHG) such as methane. In fact, the waste sector alone accounted for 6.3% of Colombia's GHG emissions in 2018 (ClimateWatch, 2021[29]). Most of this was from municipal solid waste (MSW), where Colombia produces around 18 million tonnes of organic residues (59%), plastics (13%), paper and cardboard (9%), glass (2%), metal (1%) and other wastes (16%) each year (Government of Colombia 2019[25]). About 83% of MSW is collected for disposal in landfills without further sorting, which if done would allow for greater recycling, re-use and recovery, including waste-to-energy solutions, which would reduce the environmental footprint of the sector whilst also prolonging the lifetime of landfills (RVO, 2021[30]). Indeed, if MSW were exploited fully, the technical biogas potential could reach as much as 1.4 TWh per year (Duarte, Loaiza and Majano, 2021[31]).

**Table 1.1. Technical potential for biogas production by residue type and quantity**

| Sector | Residue | Quantity | Technical potential | |
|---|---|---|---|---|
| | | *thousand tonnes/year* | *million m³/year* | *GWh*/year* |
| Livestock | Poultry manure | 2 793 | 168 | 1 000 |
| | Swine manure | 1 410 | 99 | 589 |
| | Bovine manure | 501 | 20 | 120 |
| Agriculture | Rice straw | 252 | 353 | 2 054 |
| | Banana fruit rejects | 249 | 0.4 | 2 |
| | Coffee pulp | 185 | 5 | 28 |
| | Coffee mucilage | 63 | 5 | 63 |
| | Corn stalk | 559 | 287 | 1 372 |
| | Oil palm (oxidation pond) | 6 710 | 134 | 854 |
| | Plantain fruit rejects | 117 | 0.2 | 1 |
| | Sugarcane bagasse | 6 549 | 1 | 6 294 |
| | Panela cane bagasse | 238 | <0.1 | 227 |
| Municipal | Solid urban waste (organic) | 4 278 | 282 | 724 |
| | Sludge (sewage) | 289 969 | 101 | 654 |
| Industrial | Dairy sludge and fats | 10 | 0.4 | 5 |
| | Brewery sludge | 2 | 0.1 | 1 |
| | Cane stillage | 9 587 | 158 | 902 |
| | Slaughterhouse rumen | 62 | 1 | 6 |
| **Total** | | **323 534** | **1 615** | **14 896** |

Note: GWh = gigawatt-hour. *GWh/year represents the technical energy potential for biogas production (not the electricity generation potential).
Source: adapted from (UPME, 2017[27]).

Industrial waste represents another opportunity for recovery of energy. The industry sector generates around nine million tonnes of waste each year, with a technical biogas potential of around 1 TWh (DNP, 2016[32]). This includes hazardous industrial waste such as oil, solvents and sludge, which together represented over 300 000 tonnes of waste in 2016. One third of that required special, secure landfills. Given the often high-calorific content of these types of wastes, there is a clear waste-to-energy opportunity, for instance through incineration plants and co-processing (e.g. in cement production). Waste recovery for energy production would also limit the disposal of such hazardous wastes in landfills.

In spite of the large untapped potential of available waste and residues in Colombia, use of bioenergy remains relatively limited, notably to biofuel production and to electricity and heat cogeneration in the sugarcane and palm industries. Use of technologies such as anaerobic digesters and direct use of biomass and waste (e.g. for co-processing in industry) would help to tap into this prospective, at the same time as providing a number of potential benefits such as increased access to reliable electricity in rural areas and improved energy security from reduced imports of fossil fuels. Yet, enabling widespread uptake of these bioenergy solutions will require greater awareness amongst industry and energy actors, as well as stronger policy signals such as deployment targets and use of fiscal incentives that can drive early market adoption. Encouraging uptake of bioenergy solutions will also need to take into account the government's bioeconomy and circular economy strategies (discussed in Chapter 2) to ensure that policy measures and market incentives do not encourage unsustainable bioenergy production.

### *Bioenergy can help decarbonise the energy mix, which is dominated by fossil fuels*

Energy supply and demand in Colombia are primarily met by fossil fuels, which accounted for around two-thirds of final energy consumption in 2018 (IEA, 2021[6]). The power sector may be dominated by hydro, but electricity only accounts for 18% of total energy use. Biofuels and waste[2] account for another 16%, but this is mostly traditional use of solid biomass[3] for cooking and heating in households, with smaller amounts of biomass used for cogeneration in industry as well as for biofuels in the transport sector (Figure 1.4).

Energy demand from industry and buildings accounted for just over half of final energy use in 2018 (26% and 27%, respectively), while the largest share of demand (37%) was for transportation. The transport sector was the fastest growing energy consumer over the last decade, increasing by nearly 50% between 2010 and 2018, due to rising demand for motorcycles, passenger cars and light commercial vehicles (BBVA, 2019[33]). Currently, 90% of transport energy demand is for oil, making the sector a critical driver of increased fossil fuel consumption. Fuel mandates, including requirements for 8% blend of ethanol in gasoline and a 9.2% blend of biodiesel in diesel, helped to allay some of this growth, though not nearly as quickly as transport energy demand grew since 2010. The sector's oil demand consequently reached nearly 9.5 Mtoe in 2018, eating into more than 20% of Colombia's oil production that year. Biofuels, thanks to blending requirements, represented around 7% of the sector's fuel use, with a slightly lower share (5%) of road transport energy consumption in 2018 (Rueda-Ordóñez et al., 2019[34]). This share could be further increased (e.g. with 15% ethanol and 85% gasoline [E15] blends), but changes in the current blends would be best if done in dialogue with automotive and original equipment manufacturers, as higher volume mixtures can require modifications to engines (The Royal Society, 2008[35]).

Industry, representing 26% of GDP value added (including construction), is also heavily dependent on fossil fuels, although to a lesser extent than the transport sector. Industry in Colombia includes a number of energy-intensive activities, such as coal and oil extraction, chemical products, metallurgy and cement production. Agricultural products (e.g. coffee, sugarcane, fruits and nuts) and commodities such as textiles also are important economic outputs (Santander Trade, 2021[36]). The variety in these industrial activities contributes to a greater mix in sectoral fuel use, even if fossil fuels account for around 60% of total industry energy consumption. Electricity accounts for another quarter of the sector's energy demand, and bioenergy, primarily for cogeneration with bagasse residues from Colombia's sugar and palm industries, makes up the remaining 16%. Other forms of bioenergy (e.g. biogas) from industrial or agro-industrial residues remain limited (Asocaña, 2021[37]).

The carbon intensity of industrial energy consumption has fluctuated since 2000 and was marginally lower in 2018 at 49 grammes (g) of carbon dioxide ($CO_2$) per megajoule (MJ) than in 2010 (51 $gCO_2/MJ$) (IEA,

2021[38]). This improvement is thanks to the growing share of electricity and bioenergy, which each grew by 40% and 60%, respectively, between 2010 and 2018. Part of this bioenergy growth is due to industry concerns with price volatility for oil and natural gas, while net-metering regulation (see Chapter 2) in 2015 provided additional incentive for cogeneration in the sugar and palm industries. Still, in spite of this progress, industry coal use increased by 60% during the 2010-18 period, highlighting the important role of low-cost domestic coal production in the country's reliance on this fossil fuel (IEA, 2021[6]).

**Figure 1.4. Final energy consumption by sector and fuel, 2000-18**

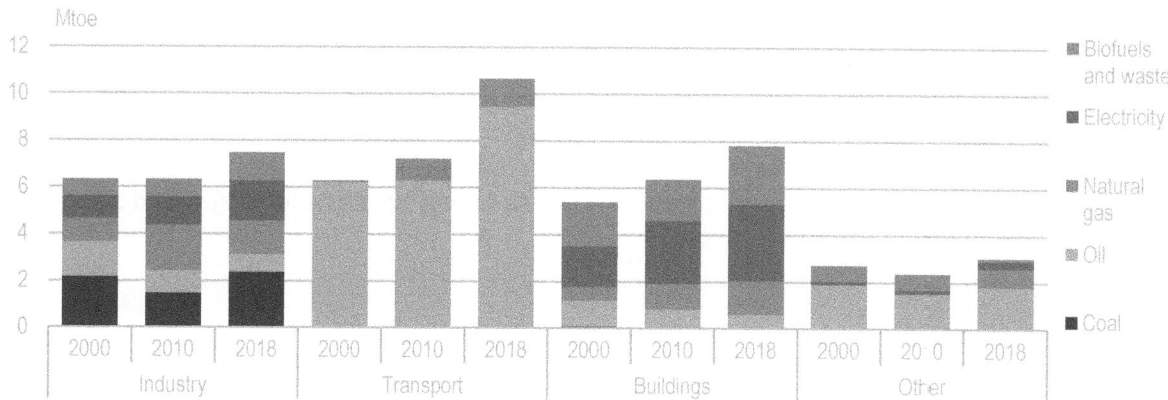


Note: "Other" includes final energy consumption in agriculture, forestry, fishing and other fuel use not elsewhere specified.[4]
Source: (IEA, 2021[6]), World Energy Balances (database).

StatLink https://stat.link/6srjt5

Buildings account for the last major share (27%) of final energy consumption, and the sector is the second fastest growing demand after transport. This is linked to steady population growth (51 million people in 2020, as compared to 45 million in 2010), increased household income and a large, growing services sector, which accounted for 57% of GDP in 2019. The latter is driven in particular by business from outsourcing and a dynamic tourism industry (World Bank, 2021[8]). The services sector, together with growing household demand, has principally contributed to strong growth in electricity use, which accounted for 42% of buildings sector energy consumption in 2018. Simultaneously, biofuels and waste (mostly in the form of traditional use of solid biomass such as firewood) accounted for around a third of buildings energy demand. In fact, while electricity use in buildings increased 20% between 2010 and 2018, biomass consumption grew by 40%. This underscores the important role that traditional use of biomass plays for heating and cooking in households, most commonly in rural populations (18.5% of the population in 2020) and in areas that do not have reliable access to the electricity grid (roughly 3.6% of the population) (IADB, 2016[39]).

The high shares of fossil fuels and traditional use of biomass in Colombia's energy mix stress the critical challenge of deploying efficient, affordable and clean energy solutions over the next decades if the country is to achieve its sustainable development goals and targeted carbon neutrality by 2050. Modern bioenergy and waste solutions can play a pivotal role in this transition, as highlighted by UPME estimates of technical potentials. Yet, policy levers will need to ensure the enabling conditions for these investments, starting first with clearer signals on the expected role renewable energy technologies will play (beyond their theoretical potential) in the country's future energy mix.

One such example of this need is illustrated by coal use in industry. Despite opportunities for clean energy uptake such as the current use of bagasse in the sugarcane industry, overall coal use in the sector increased since 2010, reversing the declining share from the early 2000s. Signals on policy expectations for industry fuel mix and/or decarbonisation pathways under the auspices of Colombia's climate commitments would help to encourage a pipeline of clean energy solutions like biomass cogeneration. Support for technology demonstration in target industries beyond sugar and palm production would also help to build the business case for bioenergy applications. These actions could be complimented by other measures such as the use of incentives like the financial assistance scheme that supports biomass-based cogeneration projects in India under the country's Ministry of New and Renewable Energy.[5]

Industry mandates and emissions trading schemes, such as those used in the European Union and the People's Republic of China (hereafter "China"), have also been successful in driving clean energy solutions like biogas and biomass cogeneration in industry. Colombia introduced a carbon tax in 2016, (Law 1819 of 2016[6]), although industry use of fuels such as coal, coke crude oil and refinery gas are not currently subject to the tax. Additionally, natural gas is only subject to the tax if used by refineries or in the petrochemical industry (OECD, 2019[40]). Addressing these exemptions, for example through an emissions trading scheme that is currently under development (Law 1931 of 2018[7]) will encourage the phase down of fossil fuel use in industry through solutions such as biomass cogeneration. Other signals, such as progressive increases in tipping fees for landfills, can similarly help to drive uptake of clean energy solutions, for instance supporting development of waste-to-energy solutions for biogas and clean electricity generation.

## Power sector development and bioenergy opportunities

Improving access to reliable and affordable electricity supply has been and continues to be a policy priority in Colombia. There has been significant restructuring of the electricity market since Law 142 of 1994 (later modified by Law 689 of 2001[8]) and Law 143[9] of 1994 were passed, allowing for private investment in generation capacity. The government has also made concerted effort to expand electricity access over the last two decades, including financial support for electricity system development, and by 2019 around 97% of the country was connected (IEA, 2020[41]). Electrification rates are highest in urban areas, covering nearly all (>99%) of the population, and the country has adequately installed capacity with respect to meeting overall electricity demand. Still, only 48% of the country (in terms of territory) has access to the national interconnected system (Sistema Interconectado Nacional), while the other 52%, representing about 1.8 to 2.2 million people, remains as non-interconnected zones (zonas no interconectadas, ZNI) (IADB, 2016[39]).

ZNI areas can lack connection to the national grid due to a number of technical, financial or environmental constraints, such as issues with transporting fuels and difficulties building transmission and distribution infrastructure. ZNI are mostly rural (89%) and are usually sparsely populated, but they can include some municipalities, cities, towns and villages that rely on isolated grids or diesel generators for electricity generation (Garces et al., 2021[42]). The challenges of expanding the national grid to these "last mile" ZNI subsequently means that distributed and off-grid solutions such as local, sustainable energy resources like bioenergy and waste can be an effective and economical opportunity to achieve full electricity access.

Elsewhere, in areas connected to the national grid, some regions rely heavily on thermal power generation using fossil fuels, in spite of Colombia's abundant hydro resources, at least on a national level. For example, Córdoba, La Guajira and Norte de Santander in the northern part of the country relied exclusively on coal for electricity generation in 2017 (OECD, 2021[43]). In fact, new coal capacity has received permits in the Córdoba and Cesar regions (Global Energy Monitor, 2021[44]), despite the high potential for solar production in those parts of the country. Given the average lifespan of a coal power plant of around 40 years, adding such new capacity would not be in line with Colombia's sustainable development targets to 2030 and beyond. The additions also point to the need to enable a robust pipeline of affordable clean energy solutions like bioenergy to compete with and substitute fossil fuel power generation in the country.

### *Secure and affordable electricity supply requires more diverse capacity*

Colombia had around 18 GW of installed power generation capacity in 2020, and the sector's carbon intensity averaged around 160 $gCO_2$/kWh over the last two decades, compared to a world average of about 475 $gCO_2$/kWh in 2018 (IEA, 2021[38]). However, this relatively low $CO_2$ intensity depends considerably on available hydropower, which represents two-thirds of total installed capacity (IEA, 2021[6]). In years of low hydro availability, coal, oil and natural gas power generation ramp up, leading to jumps in related emissions, such as the 2016 peak of 221 $gCO_2$/kWh during the El Niño cycle (Figure 1.5). More recently, power sector emissions intensity rose again in 2019 due to considerable deficits in precipitation in the first quarter of the year, underscoring growing risks from more frequent anomalies in the El Niño phenomenon and from climate change (Minambiente, 2021[45]); (Parra et al., 2020[46]).

While fossil fuels may only represent 30% of installed power generation capacity, they nevertheless play a critical role in ensuring secure supply of electricity in years of prolonged drought. At the same time, this intermittent use of those generation assets has noticeable effects on the electricity market, not just in terms of power sector emissions but also in terms of electricity spot prices. The latter is the natural consequence of sporadic need for fossil fuel capacity, which creates challenges for operators as well as for finance and capital investment in energy exploration, production and transportation (World Bank, 2019[47]). The uncertainty of weather-related events (and subsequent demand for fossil fuel power generation) also creates challenges in securing energy supply contracts, particularly as natural gas producers prefer the more stable consumption profiles of industry and the residential market.

**Figure 1.5. Share of electricity generation by fuel and resulting carbon intensity 2000-19**

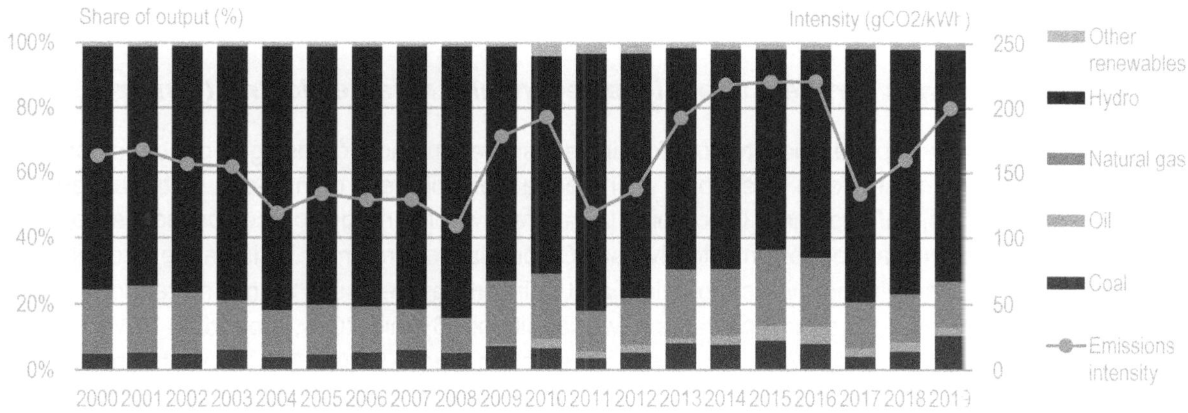


Source: (IEA, 2021[6]), World Energy Balances (database).

StatLink https://stat.link/maq2zh

The government's 2020-50 National Energy Plan (Plan Energético Nacional, PEN)[10] highlighted that growing fossil fuel imports (equivalent to 7% of national energy supply in 2020) could reach nearly 30% of Colombia's total energy supply by 2030 under a business-as-usual scenario. This would reach a staggering 69% by 2050 if left unchecked, risking costly price fluctuations and creating considerable potential energy security issues for the country (UPME, 2020[48]).

Growing reliance on fossil fuel standby increases exposure to price volatility, especially in periods when hydro capacity is diminished. To help ensure reliable and cost-effective supply of electricity during periods of drought, Colombia's energy and gas regulation commission (Comisión de Regulación de Energía y Gas, CREG) introduced a hedging mechanism in 2006 to reduce market uncertainty and to help recover a portion of fixed costs for standby power. The mechanism is based on firm power[11] obligations awarded through auctions[12] that commit generators to provide given amounts of energy at a pre-determined situational scarcity price. In return, the generators receive a fixed annual option fee, known as a reliability charge ("Cargo por Confiabilidad"), for each kWh contracted.

While in principle the reliability charge is an effective tool, a number of weaknesses were highlighted during the extreme droughts of 2016. That year was the second strongest El Niño event in the recorded history of Colombia and led to a 40% decrease in rainfall. This diminished available water in hydropower dams by as much as 60-70%. At the same time, demand for cooling and refrigeration amplified with increased temperatures, and unforeseen operational issues (including a fire that forced the outage of the 560 megawatt (MW) hydro plant in Guatapé) took another portion of remaining sources offline. This resulted in a cumulative shortage of 200 MW, more than 1% of installed capacity, in April 2016, even after taking into account successful energy saving campaigns by the government (World Energy, 2019[49]).

Thermal plants under the reliability charge subsequently kicked in, and fossil fuel power totalled around 55% of electricity produced in April 2016. This had important consequences on price stability in the market, hitting generation and distribution companies that were not adequately hedged. Scarcity prices, which were set to USD 110 per MWh, were as much as seven times lower than the actual cost of producing electricity, while the average spot price rose from around USD 30-50 to USD 400 per MWh. In fact, this higher bound was set by regulatory intervention to cap the maximum price (World Bank, 2019[47]).

A new reliability charge auction was consequently held in 2018, securing an additional 100 MW of natural gas and 260 MW of coal power to ensure higher margins of non-hydro capacity. A further renewable energy auction was planned for 2019. The extreme drought also served to push forward the renewable energy agenda as a means to diversify the power mix and address a number of the issues brought forward during the 2016 event, including growing reliance on fossil fuel imports. Much of this focus has centred on increasing wind and solar capacity additions, although bioenergy, like fossil fuel (thermal) power, has the additional potential to provide capacity on demand.

### *Clean energy solutions can help to achieve secure and reliable electricity supply*

In response to exposure to price volatility from fossil fuel generation and increasing dependence on energy imports, the government set forth intentions to increase development of non-conventional renewable energy (NCRE) sources, defined under Colombian law as renewable energy sources outside large hydro.[13] NCRE represents a significant opportunity to diversify Colombia's energy mix, for instance through greater uptake of solar, wind and bioenergy technologies, and policy measures such as net-metering regulations (see Chapter 2) have helped to spur renewable power additions. By mid-2021, around 80 MW of wind and 18 MW solar generation capacity was connected to the national grid (Figure 1.6). Small hydro accounted for another 225 MW of installed capacity, followed by 145 MW of bioenergy, mostly in the form sugarcane bagasse (141 MW) and some biogas from three anaerobic digestion plants (around 4 MW) (SIEL, 2021[50]). Altogether, these NCRE represented about 3% of total installed capacity.

Figure 1.6. Installed grid-connected power generation capacity by source, June 2021

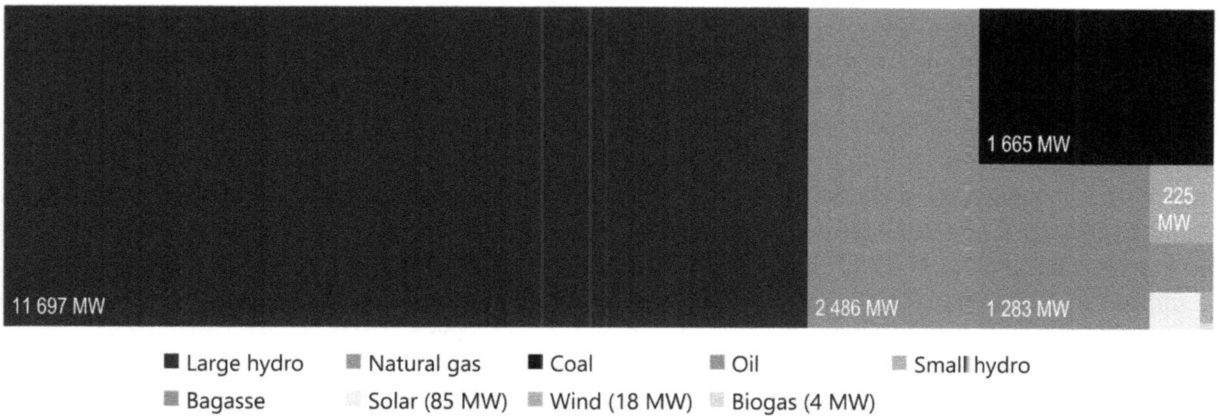


Source: (SIEL, 2021[50]) Generation Statistics Queries (database).

StatLink https://stat.link/ksgt3d

This share of NCRE is set to increase as another 2.5 GW of additions will come online in 2022, accelerated in part by the country's first successful renewable energy auctions in 2019 (Djunisic, 2020[51]). In fact, the World Economic Forum listed Colombia in its 2020 Energy Transition Index as having made the most progress on renewables in Latin America and the Caribbean, thanks in particular to the introduction of the country's first auctions (WEF, 2020[52]). Specifically, an auction was held in February 2019, although this was not successful due to issues with market concentration. A second, successful auction was then held in October of 2019, securing more than 1.3 GW of new wind and solar projects, with awarding based on competitive generation costs. These seven wind and three solar PV projects represented an estimated USD 2.2 billion of investment, primarily from large international and national players such as Trina Solar, EDP Renovables, Celsia, and Jemeiwaa Ka'I (IRENA and USAID, 2021[53]).

In addition to the auctions, UPME also approved 5.2 GW of solar and 2.5 GW of wind power additions in 2020 (Djunisic, 2020[51]). When combined with the October 2019 auction, these planned additions should add at least 2.5 GW of renewable electricity capacity by 2022, corresponding to about 12% of Colombia's expected electric power generation capacity (20 GW) by then (ITA, 2021[54]). 0.8 GW of new capacity was also awarded in a third auction held in October 2021, counting 11 solar projects worth an estimated investment of USD 875 million (Renewables Now, 2021[55]). Participants included domestic players such as Empresas Públicas de Medellín (EPM), Celsia, Empresas de Urrá and Fotovoltaica Arrayanes. There were also international developers, including the French utility EDF, the Chinese-Canadian manufacturer Canadian Solar, Italy's Enel and the Spanish solar companies Solarpack and Genersol (XM, 2021[56]). The 0.8 GW awarded should be operation in 2023 (Scully, 2021[57]).

These capacity additions in recent years have greatly supported solar and wind progress in Colombia, while by contrast, expected bioenergy additions remain limited to around 48 MW of capacity set to come online by 2022. Moreover, despite the potential for bioenergy to play a role in reducing Colombia's reliance on fossil fuels, no such capacity was awarded in the 2019 or recent 2021 auctions, even though bioenergy projects participated. This was due in part to direct competition with the diminishing costs of solar and wind power, where auctioning of electricity generation (in cost per kWh) does not necessarily capture other socio-economic benefits from bioenergy projects, such as the value of reduced waste to landfills and the ability to supply reliable electricity in areas not connected to the national grid.

Experiences in other countries, such as the "Biovalor" initiative[14] in Uruguay, highlight how bioenergy can generate local economic value whilst improving the security and reliability of energy supply. Biovalor is an initiative by the government of Uruguay, supported by the United Nations Industrial Development

Organization. Since 2016, the initiative has co-financed eight bioenergy projects, which are transforming local agricultural, industrial and municipal waste into energy and/or other bi-products such as biofertilisers (Biovalor, 2021[58]). In addition to reducing over 100 thousand tonnes of annual waste, the projects have helped to develop local technical capacity and energy technology solutions (e.g. biodigesters for micro- and small-scale production). In one project, a small biogester (12 litres of waste per day) was installed in a municipal dining hall, whose organic waste produces enough biogas to supply the kitchen's stoves for two to three hours a day, cutting the site's supergas (butane and propane) use in half. In another project, a biodigester installed at a dairy farm in the department of San José began generating around 240 kWh of electricity per day in late 2019, allowing the farm to run nearly independently during expensive peak hours and to export around 2.8 MWh of electricity per month to the national grid. Solutions similar to these could be applied in Colombia, for example in ZNI, and would help to ensure secure and reliable electricity generation through nearby available resources, with potential added benefits for local businesses.

### *Bioenergy capacity additions need a kick-start if they are to reach their potential*

Despite promising growth in bioenergy cogeneration in the mid-2010s, new capacity additions began to slow in 2017 and have since plateaued (Figure 1.7). As of June 2021, UPME's generation project registry[15] only had two proposed bioenergy projects under review, representing around 26 MW of capacity additions. By comparison, over 200 solar projects were under review, representing 11 GW of proposed additions, and a further five thermal (fossil fuel) power projects under review would add 2.6 GW of electricity generation capacity (UPME, 2021[59]).

Figure 1.7. Installed biomass cogeneration capacity, surplus and electricity sales, 2011-20

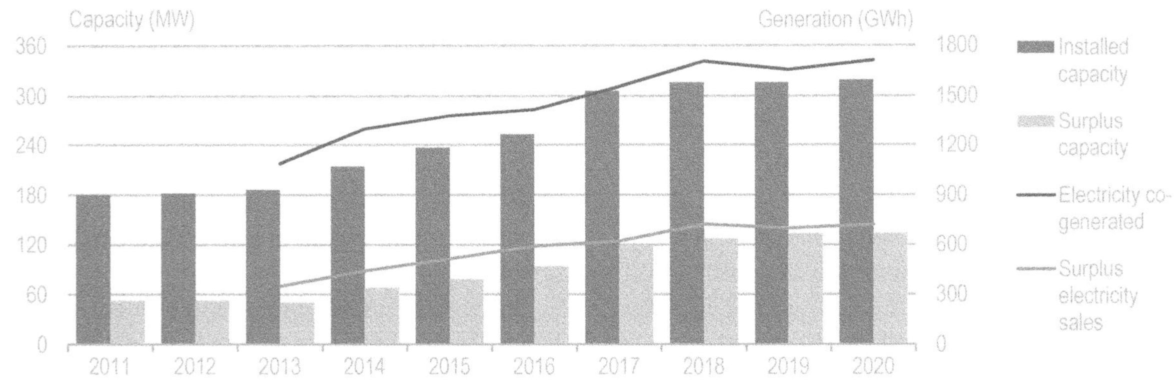


Source: adapted from (Asocaña, 2021[37]).

StatLink https://stat.link/0396te

Part of the slow-down in bioenergy project development relates to competition in pricing. The most recent UPME Reference Generation and Transmission Expansion Plan (Plan de Expansión de Referencia Generación - Transmisión) for 2020-34[16] highlighted that the average capital expenditure (capex) costs for biomass cogeneration and other bioenergy technologies were amongst the most expensive of the potential NCRE technologies (in USD per kilowatt). Additionally, experience with bioenergy developments has mostly been restricted to cogeneration in the sugarcane and palm oil industries, and even then, it is a relatively limited number of applications. As of 2021, only 13 cogeneration plants sold to the grid, representing about 150 MW of capacity (UPME, 2021[60]). Most of this capacity (eight plants) is fuelled by bagasse, and the remainder uses bagasse combined with coal or natural gas (XM, 2020[61]) (Table 1.2). Technologies like anaerobic digestion are typically at lower capex levels than other bioenergy projects such as gasification or incineration plants (Alzate-Arias et al., 2018[62]). Still, on average, the capex for bioenergy is much greater than for wind and nearly double that of solar.

## Table 1.2. Capex by technology under the UPME reference expansion plan for 2020-34

| Technology | USD per kilowatt | | |
|---|---|---|---|
| | *Minimum* | *Average* | *Maximum* |
| Coal | 1 300 | 1 900 | 2 500 |
| Oil | | 1 613 | |
| Natural gas | 1 086 | 1 150 | 1 213 |
| Large hydro | 1 704 | 1 792 | 1 880 |
| Small hydro | | 2 542 | |
| Wind | 1 108 | 1 454 | 1 800 |
| Solar | 710 | 1 105 | 1 500 |
| Bioenergy | 950 | 2 200 | 4500 |
| Biomass cogeneration | | 2 141 | |
| Geothermal | | 4 500 | |

Sources: (UPME, 2020[63]) Generation and Transmission Reference Expansion Plan 2020-2034 and OECD correspondance with UPME.

In terms of growth, the bulk of bioenergy cogeneration additions happened between 2014 and 2017, thanks notably to the passage of Law 1715 of 2014 (Colombia's Renewable Energy Law)[17] and then UPME Resolution 45 of 2016,[18] which enabled self-generators to connect to the grid. Electricity available to the grid from bagasse cogeneration consequently increased from 51 to 120 MW between 2014 and 2017 (Asocaña, 2014[64]), although this then slowed considerably, with capacity only growing a further 14 MW by 2020 (Asocaña, 2021[37]). New developments are expected to increase total capacity to around 206 MW of bagasse cogeneration connected to the grid by 2024, albeit again from the sugar and palm industries.

A few self-generation projects (industry actors with on-site power generation) using bioenergy came online in recent years, due in part to policy reforms on net-metering and also thanks to a number of tax exemptions with accelerated depreciation rules under the 2014 Renewable Energy Law. Yet, despite these, bioenergy self-generation remains uncommon, and only 2.9 MW of capacity was approved for new connections to the grid in 2021. By comparison, there were 34 MW of on-site solar PV approved for connection as self-generators (UPME, 2021[65]).

Other bioenergy generation additions remain limited to a handful of projects. Specifically, three anaerobic digestion (biogas) plants were connected to the grid in 2016, accounting for 4 MW of installed capacity (SIEL, 2021[50]). Energy in these cases is produced from wastewater treatment and landfill methane recovery. For example, the Bogotá Doña Juana biogas facility (1.7 MW) produces electricity sold to the national grid from landfill emissions. While a promising example of this sector's potential to produce grid-connected energy production, most of Colombia's industrial and municipal waste is nevertheless disposed of in one the 62 official regional landfills that do not have any further sorting or waste recovery. Low tipping (landfill) fees contribute to this lack of further treatment (RVO, 2021[30])

To address the lack of incentive to capture waste-to-energy potential, other countries have raised disposal fees, put forward more stringent policy measures limiting landfilling of waste, or applied a combination of such measures. For instance, China has taken several actions in recent years to recycle valuable wastes and reduce the amount of MSW disposed of in landfills (Zhu et al., 2020[66]) (Yan et al., 2019[67]). This has included strengthening the country's regulatory environment on MSW, increasing tipping fees and offering financial support for recycling, waste management and waste-to-energy facilities. Similar measures were taken in the European Union, where in addition to assertive regulation on landfilling, multiple regulatory, economic and administrative measures have also been used to encourage bioenergy projects (Box 1.1).

Countries have also applied more targeted measures to encourage bioenergy capacity additions. This includes measures to address bioenergy project development in the face of increasingly competitive energy sources like solar and wind power. For example, Denmark, like Colombia, has large feedstock potential from agricultural waste, in addition to competitive pricing from the country's offshore wind market. To promote bioenergy capacity additions, the government took a number of actions to encourage the production and use of those resources, including through long-term policy signals on the role biogas is expected to play in Denmark's clean energy transition to 2050. Initiatives such as subsidies for biogas projects and funding under the country's Energy Technology Development and Demonstration Programme also helped to enable rapid growth in biogas production over the last decade. In fact, by 2020, biogas already constituted about 20% of Denmark's energy supply (MoF, 2021[68]).

Enabling a strong pipeline of bioenergy and waste-to-energy projects in Colombia will require similar policy actions to encourage development and address challenges such as increasing competition with solar and wind projects. For instance, UPME can highlight the opportunity for bioenergy projects by clarifying clean energy targets through signals such as those in the European Renewable Energy Directive, which included "biomass, landfill gas, sewage treatment plant gas and biogases" as non-fossil sources under the legally binding objective to achieve 15% of energy from renewable sources. The government can also look to experiences in other countries, building upon good practices that for example enabled pre-processing and co-processing of MSW in cement production in Japan, the United States, Australia, Brazil and South Africa (Hasanbeigi et al., 2021[69]). Further measures can include working with both international and local partners to improve awareness for bioenergy solutions and to strengthen the capacity to implement them (see Annex A on the Organic recycling programme, or Reciclos Organicos).

### Box 1.1. Application of different measures encouraging bioenergy development in Europe

Legislation in the European Union discourages disposal to landfills and has been a driving force behind deployment of bioenergy solutions like anaerobic digesters, composting plants and waste incineration. Specifically, the European Union's 1999 Landfill directive[19] placed landfill disposal as the least preferable option in the waste hierarchy.[20] Landfilling of organic material is entirely banned in several countries, including Sweden, Switzerland, Austria and Germany. Landfill fees, such as the USD 132 tax per tonne of waste in the United Kingdom, also provide incentive to increase sorting, treatment and recovery for energy production.

In total, more than 700 economic, regulatory and administrative measures across the European Union were put in place between 2005 and 2017 to support bioenergy solutions such as anaerobic digestion technologies. Around 150 of these measures were financial incentives aimed at creating more favourable finance and investment conditions for biogas. Altogether, the various measures helped biogas plants in Europe to increase substantially, from around six thousand installations in 2009 to nearly 18 thousand plants in 2017.

Several European countries also combined schemes to promote deployment of bioenergy technology. This included use of feed-in tariffs, feed-in premiums, quotas, tradable certificate systems and tenders. Broadly speaking, the trend since the mid-2010s was to use capacity market mechanisms combining feed-in tariffs, feed-in premiums and tenders, for example in Germany, France, Italy and the United Kingdom. A combination of feed-in tariffs and feed-in premiums was also used in Bulgaria, Ireland, Latvia, and Croatia. At the same time, developments over the second of half of the 2010s suggest that these capacity market additions, including growing use of auctions, may have an adverse effect on bioenergy deployment, as the pace of biogas projects in Europe slowed since 2014. At the same time, this may equally be due to important shares of bioenergy in European countries' overall energy mixes, for instance in Nordic countries where waste-to-energy is rather prevalent.

European experience nevertheless highlights that clear policy signals, combined with regulatory measures, landfill pricing and other financial incentives encourage a robust pipeline of alternatives to waste disposal. These combined measures in Europe were particularly effective in encouraging early stage uptake of technology solutions like anaerobic digestion, which without this broad enabling environment would have had a far more challenging pathway to market development.

Sources: (Banja et al., 2019[70]); (Government of the United Kingdom, 2021[71]).

## References


Alzate-Arias, S. et al. (2018), "Assessment of government incentives for energy from waste in Colombia", *Sustainability (Switzerland)*, Vol. 10/4, http://dx.doi.org/10.3390/SU10041294. [62]

Asocaña (2021), *Annual Report (Informe Annual) 2020-2021*, Colombian Sugarcane Growers Association (Asociación de Cultivadores de Caña de Azúcar, Asocaña), https://www.asocana.org/documentos/1782021-3772D9B2-00FF00,000A000,878787,C3C3C3,FF00FF,2D2D2D,A3C4B5.pdf (accessed on 8 September 2021). [37]

Asocaña (2014), *The Colombian sugar sector, more than sugar, a renewable energy source for the country: co-generation (Cogeneracion - El Sector Azucarero Colombiano, más que azúcar, una fuente de energía renovable para el país)*, Colombian Sugarcane Growers Association (Asociación de Cultivadores de Caña de Azúcar, Asocaña), https://www.asocana.org/documentos/2692014-90F926BD-00FF00,000A000,878787,C3C3C3,0F0F0F,B4B4B4,FF00FF,2D2D2D.pdf (accessed on 15 September 2021). [64]

Banja, M. et al. (2019), "Support for biogas in the EU electricity sector – A comparative analysis", *Biomass and Bioenergy*, Vol. 128, p. 105313, http://dx.doi.org/10.1016/J.BIOMBIOE.2019.105313. [70]

BBVA (2019), *Colombia Automotive Outlook 2019*, BBVA Research, https://www.bbvaresearch.com/en/publicaciones/automotive-situation-colombia-2019/ (accessed on 3 August 2021). [33]

Benavides, J. and A. Cadena (2018), *Electricity market in Colombia: transition to a decentralized architecture (Mercado eléctrico en Colombia: transición hacia una arquitectura descentralizada)*, Foundation for Higher Education and Development (Fundación para la Educación Superior y el Desarrollo, Fedesarrollo), https://www.repository.fedesarrollo.org.co/bitstream/handle/11445/3673/Repor_Octubre_2018_Benavides_y_Cadena.pdf?sequence=1&isAllowed=y (accessed on 16 September 2021). [23]

Biovalor (2021), *Biovalor Project: Generating value with agro-industrial waste (Proyecto Biovalor: Generando valor con residuos agro-industriales)*, https://biovalor.gub.uy/ (accessed on 17 September 2021). [58]

ClimateWatch (2021), *Historical Greenhouse Gas Emissions: Colombia*, https://www.climatewatchdata.org/ghg-emissions?chartType=area&end_year=2018&regions=COL&start_year=1990 (accessed on 16 September 2021). [29]

Djunisic, S. (2020), *Colombia approves 7.7 GW of renewables outside of auctions*, Renewables Now, https://renewablesnow.com/news/colombia-approves-77-gw-of-renewables-outside-of-auctions-685572/ (accessed on 17 September 2021). [51]

DNP (2016), "National Council for Economic and Social Policy (Consejo Nacional de Política Económica y Social, CONPES) No. 3874", in *National Policy for the integral management of Solid Waste (Política Nacional para la gestión integral de los Residuos Sólidos)*, National Planning Department (Departamento Nacional de Planeación, DNP), Government of the Republic of Colombia. [32]

Duarte, S., B. Loaiza and A. Majano (2021), *From practice to politics: analysis of investment barriers for biogas in Colombia and measures to address them, based on the experience of developers and other relevant actors (De la práctica a la política: análisis de las barreras a la inversión en biogás en Colombia y las medidas para abordarlas, a partir de la experiencia de los desarrolladores y otros actores relevantes)*, LEDS-LAC, https://ledslac.org/wp-content/uploads/2021/08/Informe-final-biogas-Colombia-v.06082021-final.pdf (accessed on 16 September 2021). [31]

EFE (2021), *Foreign investment boosts renewable energy in Colombia (La inversión extranjera impulsa las energías renovables en Colombia)*, https://www.efe.com/efe/america/economia/la-inversion-extranjera-impulsa-las-energias-renovables-en-colombia/20000011-4577328 (accessed on 3 September 2021). [4]

EIA (2020), *Colombia*, United States Energy Information Administration (EIA), https://www.eia.gov/international/data/country/COL (accessed on 27 August 2021). [7]

FAO (2003), *Review of World Water Resources by Country*, Food and Agriculture Organization (FAO) of the United Nations, http://www.fao.org/publications/card/en/c/Y4473E/ (accessed on 3 September 2021). [11]

Garces, E. et al. (2021), "Lessons from last mile electrification in Colombia: Examining the policy framework and outcomes for sustainability", *Energy Research & Social Science* Vol. 79, pp. 102-156, http://dx.doi.org/10.1016/J.ERSS.2021.102156. [42]

Global Energy Monitor (2021), *Global Coal Plant Tracker*, https://endcoal.org/global-coal-plant-tracker/ (accessed on 21 September 2021). [44]

Government of Colombia (2019), *National Circular Economy Strategy Content: closing of material cycles, technological innovation, collaboration and new business models (Estrategia Nacional de Economía Circular Contenido: cierre de ciclos de materiales, innovación tecnológica, colaboración y nuevos modelos de negocio)*, Ministry of Environment and Sustainable Development (Ministerio de Ambiente y Desarrollo Sostenible) and Ministry of Commerce, Trade and Tourism (Ministerio de Comercio, Industria y Turismo), http://www.andi.com.co/Uploads/Estrategia%20Nacional%20de%20EconA%CC%83%C2%B3mia%20Circular-2019%20Final.pdf_637176135049017259.pdf (accessed on 16 September 2021). [25]

Government of the United Kingdom (2021), *Landfill Tax Rates*, HM Revenue & Customs, https://www.gov.uk/government/publications/rates-and-allowances-landfill-tax/landfill-tax-rates-from-1-april-2013 (accessed on 4 October 2021). [71]

Hasanbeigi, A. et al. (2021), *International best practices for pre-processing and co-processing municipal solid waste and sewage sludge in the cement industry*, Lawrence Berkeley National Laboryator, https://www.eceee.org/library/conference_proceedings/eceee_Industrial_Summer_Study/2012/2-sustainable-production-design-and-supply-chain-initiatives/international-best-practices-for-pre-processing-and-co-processing-municipal-solid-waste-and-sewage-sludge-in-the-cement-industry/ (accessed on 17 September 2021). [69]

IADB (2016), *Colombia: Renewable Energy Financing Program for the Non-Interconnected Zones*, Inter-American Development Bank (IADB), Washington, D.C., https://www.greenfinancelac.org/wp-content/uploads/2016/09/PP__Project_Profile.pdf (accessed on 17 September 2021). [39]

IDEAM (2020), *Average wind speed at 10 meters above sea level (Velocidad promedio del viento a 10 metros de altura)*, Institute of Hydrology, Meteorology and Environmental Studies (Instituto de Hidrología, Meteorología y Estudios Ambientales, IDEAM), http://atlas.ideam.gov.co/visorAtlasVientos.html (accessed on 3 September 2021). [15]

IDEAM (2020), *Daily mean horizontal global irradiation (Irradiacion global horizontal media diaria)*, Institute of Hydrology, Meteorology and Environmental Studies (Instituto de Hidrología, Meteorología y Estudios Ambientales, IDEAM), http://atlas.ideam.gov.co/visorAtlasRadiacion.html (accessed on 3 September 2021). [20]

IEA (2021), *Energy Transitions Indicators*, International Energy Agency (IEA), https://www.iea.org/reports/energy-transitions-indicators (accessed on 3 September 2021). [38]

IEA (2021), *World Energy Balances*, International Energy Agency (IEA), https://www.iea.org/data-and-statistics/data-product/world-energy-balances (accessed on 3 September 2021). [6]

IEA (2020), *SDG7: Data and Projections*, International Energy Agency (IEA), Paris, https://www.iea.org/reports/sdg7-data-and-projections (accessed on 21 September 2021). [41]

IEA (2017), *Technology Roadmap: Delivering Sustainable Bioenergy*, International Energy Agency (IEA), Paris, https://www.iea.org/reports/technology-roadmap-delivering-sustainable-bioenergy (accessed on 8 November 2021). [24]

IHA (2020), *Country profile: Colombia*, International Hydropower Association (IHA), https://www.hydropower.org/country-profiles/colombia (accessed on 16 September 2021). [12]

IRENA (2020), *Renewable Energy and Jobs: Annual Review 2020*, International Renewable Energy Agency, https://www.irena.org/-/media/files/IRENA/Agency/Publication/2020/Sep/IRENA_RE_Jobs_2020.pdf (accessed on 16 September 2021). [28]

IRENA (2020), *Statistics Time Series*, International Renewable Energy Agency (IRENA), https://www.irena.org/Statistics/View-Data-by-Topic/Capacity-and-Generation/Statistics-Time-Series (accessed on 16 September 2021). [19]

IRENA and USAID (2021), *Renewable energy auctions in Colombia: context, design and results*, International Renewable Energy Agency (IRENA) and United States Agency for International Development (USAID), https://www.irena.org/publications/2021/March/Renewable-energy-auctions-in-Colombia. [53]

ITA (2021), *Colombia - Country Commercial Guide*, International Trade Administration (ITA), United States Department of Commerce, https://www.trade.gov/knowledge-product/exporting-colombia-market-overview (accessed on 16 September 2021). [2]

ITA (2021), *Energy Resource Guide - 2021 Edition: Colombia - Renewable Energy*, International Trade Administration (ITA), United States Department of Commerce, https://www.trade.gov/energy-resource-guide-colombia-renewable-energy-2 (accessed on 17 September 2021). [54]

López, A. et al. (2020), "Solar PV generation in Colombia: a qualitative and quantitative approach to analyze the potential of solar energy market", *Renewable Energy*, Vol. 148, pp. 1266-1279, http://dx.doi.org/10.1016/J.RENENE.2019.10.066. [21]

Minambiente (2021), *The El Niño phenomenon is already impacting Colombia (El fenómeno de El Niño ya está impactando Colombia)*, Ministry of Environment and Sustainable Development (Ministerio de Ambiente y Desarrollo Sostenible), https://www.minambiente.gov.co/index.php/noticias/4234-el-fenomeno-de-el-nino-ya-esta-impactando-colombia-minambiente (accessed on 21 September 2021). [45]

MoF (2021), *Go green with the strong bioenergy industry in Denmark*, Ministry of Foreign Affairs (MoF), Government of Denmark, https://investindk.com/set-up-a-business/cleantech/bioenergy (accessed on 17 September 2021). [68]

Mordor Intelligence (2020), *Colombia wind energy warket: growth, trends, COVID-19 impact, and forecasts (2021-2026)*, Mordor Intelligence, https://www.mordorintelligence.com/industry-reports/colombia-wind-energy-market (accessed on 3 September 2021). [14]

Norton Rose Fulbright (2016), *Renewable energy in Latin America*, https://www.nortonrosefulbright.com/en/knowledge/publications/b09be352/renewable-energy-in-latin-america-colombia (accessed on 6 July 2021). [13]

OECD (2021), *Colombia: Progress in the net zero transition*, https://www.oecd.org/regional/RO2021%20Colombia.pdf (accessed on 21 September 2021). [43]

OECD (2019), *Taxing Energy Use 2019: Country Note – Colombia*, Organisation for Economic Co-operation and Development (OECD), Paris, http://oecd.org/tax/tax-policy/taxing-energy-use-colombia.pdf (accessed on 6 January 2022). [40]

Parra, L. et al. (2020), "Assessing the Complementarities of Colombia's Renewable Power Plants", *Frontiers in Energy Research*, p. 280, http://dx.doi.org/10.3389/FENRG.2020.575240. [46]

Pedrick, J. (ed.) (2020), *Colombia LNG imports rise on drought-depleted hydropower reservoirs*, S&P Global Platts, https://www.spglobal.com/platts/en/market-insights/latest-news/electric-power/051920-colombia-lng-imports-rise-on-drought-depleted-hydropower-reservoirs (accessed on 3 September 2021). [10]

Procolombia (2021), *Non-conventional energy sources | Invest in Colombia*, The Renewable Energy Sector in Colombia, https://investincolombia.com.co/en/sectors/energy/renewable-energy (accessed on 3 September 2021). [5]

REN21 (2014), *Renewables 2014: Global Status Report*, REN21, https://www.ren21.net/wp-content/uploads/2019/05/GSR2014_Full-Report_English.pdf (accessed on 16 September 2021). [22]

Renewables Now (2021), *Solar projects for 796.3 MW win in Colombia's renewables auction*, News, https://renewablesnow.com/news/solar-projects-for-7963-mw-win-in-colombias-renewables-auction-758784/ (accessed on 30 November 2021). [55]

Reuters (2021), "Life expectancy for Colombia's proven oil reserves closed 2020 stable at 6.3 years", https://www.reuters.com/business/energy/life-expectancy-colombias-proven-oil-reserves-closed-2020-stable-63-years-2021-06-01/ (accessed on 3 September 2021). [9]

Rueda-Ordóñez, D. et al. (2019), "Environmental and economic assessment of the co-firing of the coal-bagassemixture in the Colombian sugarcane mills", *Revista UIS Ingenierías*, Vol. 18/2, pp. 77-88, http://dx.doi.org/10.18273/REVUIN.V18N2-2019007. [34]

RVO (2021), *Waste Management in the LATAM Region: Business Opportunities for the Netherlands in waste/circular economy sector in eight countries of Latin America*, The Netherlands Enterprise Agency (RVO), https://www.rvo.nl/sites/default/files/2021/02/Report_LATAM_Waste_Management_feb_2021.pdf (accessed on 16 September 2021). [30]

Santander Trade (2021), *Colombian economic outline*, https://santandertrade.com/en/portal/analyse-markets/colombia/economic-outline (accessed on 17 September 2021). [36]

Scully, J. (2021), "Colombia awards 800MW of solar in third renewables auction - PV Tech", *PV Tech*, https://www.pv-tech.org/colombia-awards-800mw-of-solar-in-third-renewables-auction/ (accessed on 29 November 2021). [57]

SIEL (2021), *Generation Statistics Queries (Consultas Estadísticas de Generación) (database)*, Colombian Electrical Information System (Sistema de Informacion Eléctrico Colombiano), http://www.siel.gov.co/Inicio/Generaci%C3%B3n/Generaci%C3%B3n1/tabid/143/Default.aspx (accessed on 16 September 2021). [50]

The Royal Society (2008), *Sustainable biofuels: prospects and challenges*, https://royalsociety.org/topics-policy/publications/2008/sustainable-biofuels/ (accessed on 17 September 2021). [35]

Universidad Nacional de Colombia (ed.) (2017), *Estimation of the potential for biogas conversion from biomass in Colombia and its use (Estimaciòn del potencial de conversiòn a biogàs de la biomasa en Colombia y su aprovechamiento)*, Planning Unit of the Ministry of Mines and Energy (Unidad de Planeación Minero Energética, UPME), http://bdigital.upme.gov.co/jspui/handle/001/1317 (accessed on 17 September 2021). [27]

UPME (2021), *(Project Registry) Registro de proyectos*, Mining and Energy Planning Unit (Unidad de Planeación Minero Energética), https://www1.upme.gov.co/Paginas/Registro.aspx (accessed on 7 October 2021). [59]

UPME (2021), *Effective generation capacity (Capacidad efectiva de generación)*, Planning Unit of the Ministry of Mines and Energy (Unidad de Planeación Minero Energética, UPME), http://www.upme.gov.co/Reports/Default.aspx?ReportPath=%2fSIEL+UPME%2fGeneraci%u00f3n%2fCapacidad+Efectiva+de+Generaci%u00f3n+(SIN) (accessed on 17 September 2021). [60]

UPME (2021), *Self-generation and distributed generation requests 2021 (Solicitudes de autogeneración y generación distribuida 2021)*, Planning Unit of the Ministry of Mines and Energy (Unidad de Planeación Minero Energética, UPME), https://public.tableau.com/app/profile/upme/viz/AutogeneracionyGeneracionDistribuida2021/Historia1 (accessed on 17 September 2021). [65]

UPME (2020), *Generation and Transmission Reference Expansion Plan 2020-2034 (Plan de expansión de referencia generación – transmisión 2020-2034)*, Planning Unit of the Ministry of Mines and Energy (Unidad de Planeación Minero Energética, UPME), http://www.siel.gov.co/Inicio/Generaci%c3%b3n/PlanesdeExpansi%c3%b3nGeneraci%c3%b3nTransmisi%c3%b3n/tabid/111/Default.aspx (accessed on 17 September 2021). [63]

UPME (2020), *National Energy Plan 2020-2050 (Plan Energético Nacional 2020-2050)*, Planning Unit of the Ministry of Mines and Energy (Unidad de Planeación Minero Energética, UPME), http://www1.upme.gov.co/DemandayEficiencia/Documents/PEN_2020_2050/Plan_Energetico_Nacional_2020_2050.pdf (accessed on 17 September 2021). [48]

UPME (2015), *Integration of non-conventional renewable energy in Colombia (Integración de las energías renovables no convencionales en Colombia)*, Planning Unit of the Ministry of Mines and Energy (Unidad de Planeación Minero Energética, UPME), http://www.upme.gov.co/Estudios/2015/Integracion_Energias_Renovables/INTEGRACION_ENERGIAS_RENOVANLES_WEB.pdf (accessed on 16 September 2021). [16]

UPME (2011), *Atlas of the energy potential of residual biomass in Colombia (Atlas del potencial energético de la Biomasa residual en Colombia)*, Planning Unit of the Ministry of Mines and Energy (Unidad de Planeación Minero Energética, UPME), https://www1.upme.gov.co/siame/Paginas/atlas-del-potencial-energetico-de-la-biomasa.aspx (accessed on 3 September 2021). [26]

Vesga, I. (2021), *Colombia Has High Potential for Renewable Energy*, Holland and Knight, https://www.hklaw.com/en/insights/publications/2021/03/colombia-has-high-potential-for-renewable-energy (accessed on 6 July 2021). [17]

WEF (2020), *Energy Transition Index 2020: from crisis to rebound*, World Economic Forum (WEF), https://www.weforum.org/reports/fostering-effective-energy-transition-2020 (accessed on 17 September 2021). [52]

WITS (2021), *Colombia Trade*, World Integrated Trade Solution (WITS), https://wits.worldbank.org/countrysnapshot/en/col/textview (accessed on 16 September 2021). [1]

World Bank (2021), *Foreign direct investment, net inflows (% of GDP)*, International Monetary Fund, International Financial Statistics and Balance of Payments databases, World Bank, International Debt Statistics, and World Bank and OECD GDP estimates, https://data.worldbank.org/indicator/BX.KLT.DINV.WD.GD.ZS?end=2019&start=1995 (accessed on 1 October 2021). [3]

World Bank (2021), *World Bank Development Indicators (database)*, World Bank, https://databank.worldbank.org/source/world-development-indicators. [8]

World Bank (2020), *Solar resource maps of Germany*, Global Solar Atlas 2.0, https://solargis.com/maps-and-gis-data/download/germany (accessed on 16 September 2021). [18]

World Bank (2019), *Learning from Developing Country Power Market Experiences : The Case of Colombia*, World Bank Group, Washington DC, https://documents.worldbank.org/en/publication/documents-reports/documentdetail/898231552316685139/learning-from-developing-country-power-market-experiences-the-case-of-colombia (accessed on 27 August 2021). [47]

World Energy (2019), *Case study series - Extreme Weather: El Niño, Colombia 2015/16*, World Energy Council, https://www.worldenergy.org/assets/downloads/El_ni%C3%B1o_Colombia_-Extreme_weather_conditions_SEP2019.pdf (accessed on 6 July 2021). [49]

XM (2021), *Results of auction CLPE-03 2021 (Resultados subasta CLPE-03 2021)*, Auctions (Subasta), https://www.xm.com.co/SubastaCLPE2021/Informe%20Resultados%20Nueva%20Subasta%202021.pdf (accessed on 30 November 2021). [56]

XM (2020), *Monitoring Report - Co-generators (Informe Seguimiento Cogeneradores)*, Market Experts Company (Compañía Expertos en Mercados, XM), https://www.xm.com.co/Informe%20Trimestral%20de%20Seguimiento%20a%20Cogeneradores/2021/INFORME_COGENERADORES_Julio_2021.pdf (accessed on 17 September 2021). [61]

Yan, M. et al. (2019), "Municipal Solid Waste Management and Treatment in China", *Sustainable Waste Management Challenges in Developing Countries*, pp. 86-114, http://dx.doi.org/10.4018/978-1-7998-0198-6.CH004. [67]

Zhu, Y. et al. (2020), "A review of municipal solid waste in China: characteristics, compositions, influential factors and treatment technologies", *Environment, Development and Sustainability 2020 23:5*, Vol. 23/5, pp. 6603-6622, http://dx.doi.org/10.1007/S10668-020-00959-9. [66]

## Notes

[1] For more information (in Spanish), see: https://www.minenergia.gov.co/plan-5-caribe.

[2] Biofuels and waste can include: primary solid biofuels such as firewood; biogases; municipal waste (renewable and non-renewable) and industrial waste; charcoal and other biofuels (e.g. biogasoline, biodiesel and other liquid biofuels). For more information on the product definitions by the International Energy Agency, see: http://wds.iea.org/wds/pdf/WORLDBAL_Documentation.pdf.

[3] Traditional use of biomass refers to the combustion of wood, animal waste and traditional charcoal. For more information: https://www.irena.org/bioenergy.

[4] For more information see the database documentation for the International Energy Agency's *World Energy Balances*: http://wds.iea.org/wds/pdf/WORLDBAL_Documentation.pdf.

[5] For more information, see: https://mnre.gov.in/bio-energy/schemes.

[6] For more information, see: https://www.funcionpublica.gov.co/eva/gestornormativo/norma.php?i=79140

[7] For more information, see: https://www.funcionpublica.gov.co/eva/gestornormativo/norma.php?i=87765

[8] For more information (in Spanish), see: https://www.funcionpublica.gov.co/eva/gestornormativo/norma.php?i=4633.

[9] For more information (in Spanish), see: https://www.funcionpublica.gov.co/eva/gestornormativo/norma.php?i=4631.

[10] For more information (in Spanish), see: http://www1.upme.gov.co/DemandayEficiencia/Documents/PEN_2020_2050/Plan_Energetico_Nacional_2020_2050.pdf.

[11] Firm power obligations are commitment to deliver electricity and/or heat (power) at all times during the period covered by the terms of the auction, even under adverse conditions.

[12] Auctions are governed by Article 2 of CREG Resolution 71 of 2006. For more information (in Spanish), see: http://apolo.creg.gov.co/Publicac.nsf/Indice01/Resolucion-2006-Creg071-2006

[13] Non-conventional renewable energy (NCRE) sources, or *'Fuentes No Convencionales de Energía Renovable'*, was defined in Article 5 of Law 1715 of 2014 (the "Renewable Energy Law") and include bioenergy, small-scale hydro, wind, geothermal, solar and tidal power. For more information on Law 1715 (in Spanish), see: http://www.secretariasenado.gov.co/senado/basedoc/ley_1715_2014.html.

[14] For more information (in Spanish), see: https://biovalor.gub.uy/.

[15] For more information (in Spanish), see: http://www.siel.gov.co/Inicio/Generaci%C3%B3n/Inscripci%C3%B3ndeproyectosdeGeneraci%C3%B3n/tabid/113/Default.aspx.

[16] For more information (in Spanish), see: http://www.upme.gov.co/Docs/Plan_Expansion/2020/Volumen3_Plan_Expansion_Generacion_Transmision_2020_2034_Final.pdf.

[17] For more information (in Spanish), see: http://www.minminas.gov.co/documents/10180//23517//22602-11506.pdf.

[18] For more information (in Spanish), see: https://www.incp.org.co/Site/2016/info/archivos/resolucion-045-minminas.pdf.

[19] More information available: https://eur-lex.europa.eu/legal-content/EN/TXT/?uri=CELEX:31999L0031.

[20] More information available: https://ec.europa.eu/environment/topics/waste-and-recycling/waste-framework-directive_en.

# 2 Planning and governance for bioenergy development

Colombia's ambitious decarbonisation targets are supported by a number of national policy strategies, such as the Green Growth Policy (Política de Crecimiento Verde) and the forthcoming energy transition policy (Política de Transición Energética). Yet, fossil fuels still account for over half of energy supply outlooks to 2050. A clearer strategy for Colombia's clean energy transition is therefore needed to encourage finance and investment in renewable energy solutions. This includes reflecting long-term power sector needs and opportunities within short- to medium-term generation expansion plans, which do not currently reflect the technical or socio-economic value of potential clean energy solutions like biomethane electricity production. Additional measures such as a more streamlined planning and approval process for power generation projects can equally help reduce barriers to bioenergy development.

## Highlights

- Colombia has put forward a number of national policy strategies that emphasise the country's commitment to climate action, but bioenergy opportunities, beyond high-level mentions, are not spelled out clearly in energy transition plans to 2050.
- The cross-sectoral nature of bioenergy projects can involve multiple actors and various regulations, making for a complex policy environment for developers to navigate. Improved planning and co-ordination across government authorities and relevant stakeholders will help to identify and streamline barriers to bioenergy projects.
- While decarbonisation is highlighted as a priority in national energy plans, fossil fuels still account for as much as 55% to 66% of energy supply to 2050. Spelling out a clear strategy on how the government plans to achieve the clean energy transition and its emissions reduction targets will encourage development and investment in bioenergy solutions such as biogas.
- Reliance on current project pipelines in the Reference Generation and Transmission Expansion Plan does not reflect the technical opportunities or socio-economic value of potential clean energy solutions like biomethane electricity production. Generation plans can do more to reflect policy ambitions using techno-economic models that consider how to meet power system needs in the most efficient or acceptable manner, as is often done in other countries.
- The multi-year approval process for electricity generation projects and grid connection can be a barrier for bioenergy projects, particularly for smaller developers that may need support to navigate multiple policy environments. Shortening lead times and facilitating the planning and approval process can help create an early pipeline of bioenergy projects and attract greater interest in developing future capacity additions.

Colombia only represents around 0.5% of global greenhouse gas (GHG) emissions (ClimateWatch, 2021[1]), but the country has nevertheless set ambitious emissions reduction targets in its recently revised Nationally Determind Contibutions (NDC) under the Paris Agreement, aiming to cut emissions by 51% by 2030 with appropriate international funding support (Climate Action Tracker, 2021[2]). That target is up from the 30% previously indicated in Colombia's 2015 NDC (Government of Colombia, 2015[3]), demonstrating the country's commitment to climate action on the international stage. The update also aligns more closely with ambitions to achieve carbon neutrality by 2050, as set forth by the Ministry of Environment and Sustainable Development (Ministerio de Ambiente y Desarrollo Sostenible, MADS) in its long-term strategy to face climate change (MADS, 2020[4]).

To achieve these emissions reduction targets, Colombia has a number of national policy strategies touching upon the country's clean energy transition, including the government's 2018 Green Growth Policy (Política de Crecimiento Verde),[1] the 2019 National Circular Economy Strategy (Estrategia Nacional de Economía Circular),[2] and a forthcoming energy transition policy (expected in late 2021). Given Colombia's abundant bioenergy resources, the strategies take note of the role these solutions can play in supporting decarbonisation objectives through fossil fuel substitution (e.g. through biogas production), whilst also addressing the environmental impact of Colombia's waste streams.

At the same time, Colombia's strategic policy still includes a notable reliance on fossil fuels in the country's long-term energy vision to 2050, and bioenergy mentions, while noted, remain relatively high level and non-specific. A clearer indication would thus help to set forth the role these opportunities are expected to play in reducing emissions to 2050, particularly given the more complex nature of bioenergy projects (e.g. in sourcing, sorting and treatment of waste). A more strategic policy framework for bioenergy would also help to tailor any measures or policy support to stimulate market growth, for example for solutions like biogas and biomethane production that have yet to gain real traction. This type of national strategy for bioenergy development would equally encourage a more coherent institutional framework, especially given the number of actors and policies that touch upon agricultural, industrial and municipal waste streams.

## Increasing institutional co-ordination will facilitate bioenergy development

Colombia's clean energy transition and the potential role for bioenergy to diversify the country's energy mix are touched upon in a number of national strategies set forth by the National Council for Social and Economic Policy (Consejo Nacional de Política Económica y Social, CONPES). These strategies, co-ordinated by the National Planning Department (Departamento Nacional de Planeación, DNP), provide an overarching planning framework to evaluate and direct policy priorities across government bodies, where DNP is the executive administrative agency in charge of leading, co-ordinating and defining inter-sectoral public and economic policy.

The Ministry of Mines and Energy (Ministerio de Minas y Energía, MME) is then the primary authority for the energy sector, whilst a number of other government bodies also influence the energy market and policy related to bioenergy and waste (Figure 2.1). For example, MME oversees regulation of the electricity market, but the Energy and Gas Regulation Commission (Comisión de Regulación de Energía y Gas CREG), sets the rules and roles for participating agents in the electricity market. CREG also sets eligibility criteria for non-conventional renewable energy (NCRE) incentives, including for related bioenergy projects.

Figure 2.1. Authorities influencing national bioenergy governance in Colombia

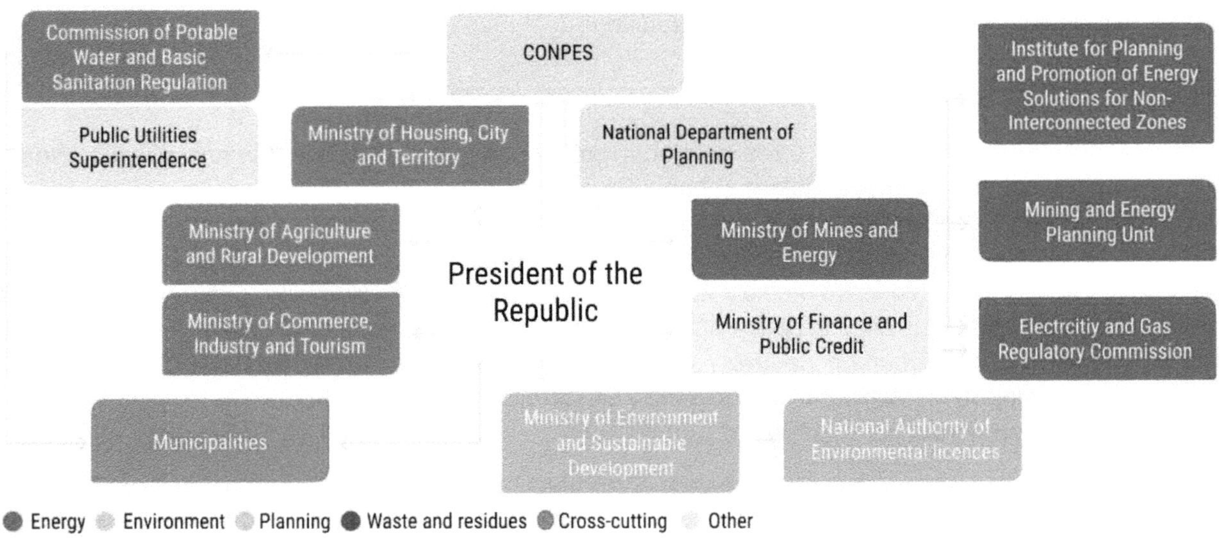


Note: the table only reflects governance at the national level and does not account for subnational authorities influencing bioenergy.
Source: Adapted from (OECD, 2021[5])

The Planning Unit of the Ministry of Mines and Energy (Unidad de Planeación Minero Energética UPME), oversees and determines the country's long-term energy strategy, including importantly the National Energy Plan (PEN), which established long-term scenarios for renewable energy development. UPME also sets short- to medium-term energy strategies for NCRE development via its Reference Generation and Transmission Expansion Plan, and part of this is touched upon by the Institute of Planning and Promotion of Energy Solutions in Non-Interconnected Zones (Instituto de Planificación y Promoción de Soluciones Energéticas para Zonas No Interconectadas, IPSE). Specifically, IPSE plans, identifies, implements and monitors sustainable energy solutions for Non-interconnected Zones (ZNI).

The wide scope of bioenergy and waste means several other ministries influence the policy framework for these projects. For example, the Ministry of Agriculture and Rural Development (Ministerio de Agricultura y Desarrollo Rural) oversees rural and agricultural policy, whilst the Ministry of Housing, City and Territory (Ministerio de Vivienda, Ciudad y Territorio) is in charge of urban planning policy, including water, waste and sanitation services. The Ministry of Commerce, Industry and Tourism (Ministerio de Comercio, Industria y Turismo) also influences potential bioenergy use, for example through its industry policy and regulations. Additionally, MADS and the National Authority of Environmental Licences (Autoridad Nacional de Licencias Ambientales) are responsible for any related environmental policy and licencing.

MADS and the Ministry of Housing, City and Territory are two particularly important ministries given their role in overseeing waste streams (including collaboration with the Ministry of Agriculture on organic waste) that are the feedstock for bioenergy projects. For example, the Ministry of Housing oversees the Superintendence of Residential Public Services (Superintendencia de Servicios Públicos Domiciliarios) and the Regulation Commission of Potable Water and Basic Sanitation (Comisión de Regulación de Agua Potable y Saneamiento), which each regulate waste management entities as well as the design and implementation of related policy, such as municipal waste tariffs at landfills. MADS similarly oversees environmental policies related to Colombia's extended producer responsibility programme,[3] which works with industry to improve end-of-lifecycle management of post-consumer waste, such as plastic packaging, batteries and tyres. This, of course, also touches upon policies and regulations overseen by the Ministry of Commerce, Industry and Tourism.

Given the cross-sectoral nature of bioenergy opportunities (e.g. touching on landfill disposal and industry policy), progress on project development can be hindered, in part, by the large number of actors involved, without these necessarily being well co-ordinated. There are currently no mechanisms in place to ensure that ministry objectives and resultant policy frameworks on waste streams and bioenergy development are aligned (DNP, 2018[6]). Enforcement and monitoring can also fall under different authorities at both the national and subnational levels. For instance, municipalities are directly responsible for the design and implementation of their own 12-year waste management plans (planes de gestión integral de residuos sólidos) (RVO, 2021[7]). Yet, these plans do not include considerations for energy recovery, despite allusions to bioenergy and circular economy opportunities in national policy. Varying local regulatory conditions with multiple responsible authorities can also make it challenging for alternative waste treatment solutions to emerge, as developers have to navigate the complex policy environment affecting the chain of activities related to bioenergy projects (Chambers and Partners, 2020[8]). This can add layers of complexity for project development, for instance in acquiring permits and licences. In practice, it also has led to waste being transported long distances to be disposed of in other landfills, rather than employing it as an alternative local energy solution.

Indeed, the juxtaposition of relevant authorities is evident in the government's recent Bioeconomy Strategy,[4] which was developed in participation with no less than six ministries, alongside DNP, the Presidential Council for Competitiveness and Public-Private Management (Consejería Presidencial para la Competitividad y la Gestión Pública-Privada) and several other partners (Government of Colombia, 2020[9]). The strategy outlines a number of important objectives and opportunities to support achievement of the government's vision for a competitive bioeconomy, but it falls short of outlining how these actions will be co-ordinated across the relevant authorities. In fact, the 2018 Green Growth Policy and the 2019 National Circular Economy Strategy both highlighted this issue, emphasising that the untapped potential of waste stream recovery for energy production will require strengthened institutional co-ordination.

To support a robust pipeline of bioenergy development and open the door to investment opportunities in these projects, the government should build upon its ambitious clean energy and bioeconomy strategies with greater planning and co-ordination across relevant government institutions and related stakeholders. This would help to identify and streamline barriers in the regulatory environment for bioenergy and waste-to-energy projects, whilst equally improving use of national and subnational government resources in support of project development. Increased dialogues across public and private stakeholders will also help co-ordinate activities to identify and support viable projects. Such co-ordination could be led by DNP, in its role on managing inter-sectoral public and economic policy, or possibly through a special task force across key actors, such as those involved in the 2020 Bioenergy Strategy.

One such example of said co-operation for bioenergy development is the Inter-institutional Bioenergy Table that was created in Ecuador. The table was created to co-ordinate actions across several policy authorities in order to identify and implement measures that enable development of activities related to bioenergy, including creation of new value chains and measures that have a positive impact on the country's trade balance.[5] A similar task group known as the Biobased Products and Bioenergy Co-ordination Council[6] was formed in the United States in 2013. This council provided a forum under the Department of Agriculture for government agencies to co-ordinate, facilitate and promote biobased products and bioenergy from agricultural and forestry materials.

## Strategic planning can spell out the opportunities for bioenergy projects

UPME's PEN set the long-term framework for national energy policy and outlined four energy pathways to 2050, based on increasing degrees of decarbonisation through penetration of renewable and energy-efficient technologies, as well as through elements of changing consumer behaviour (Figure 2.2). These pathways range from the business-as-usual trajectory ("actualisation"), continuing current market and policy trends, to a "disruption" scenario with technology breakthroughs that would achieve deeper levels of emissions reduction, with a particular focus on penetration of green hydrogen. In between, the "modernisation" scenario places specific focus on natural gas as a transition fuel, and the "inflection" scenario focuses on increasing electrification with greater penetration of renewables (including bioenergy, offshore wind and geothermal technologies) as well as some nuclear energy.

Under the actualisation scenario, energy demand is set to grow by 48% over 2019 levels, driven in particular by projected economic growth and continued rise in household income. Strong reliance on coal and oil leads to 55% growth in energy-related emissions by 2050 over 2019 levels, while in the modernisation scenario, expanded use of natural gas and liquefied petroleum gas help to transition energy demand away from coal, in line with currently stated policy ambitions. Still, energy-related emissions continue to increase in the modernisation scenario, even if less sharply than in the actualisation case. Neither pathway thereby aligns with Colombia's NDC to 2030 nor with the government's long-term decarbonisation ambitions.

The inflection and disruption scenarios require a more substantial change in energy policy priorities. This includes greater levels of renewable energy penetration as well as support to develop and deploy "disruptive" technologies such as carbon capture and storage. Both alternative pathways see emissions reduced compared to the actualisation scenario to 2050 (by 23% and 41%, respectively), in part because of lesser growth in energy demand (e.g. through energy efficiency measures) and due to use of renewable energy sources (alongside greater electrification). Yet, only the disruption scenario leads to an absolute reduction (19%) in energy-related emissions relative to the 2019 baseline. This scenario also relies heavily on deployment of green (renewable) hydrogen production.

Whereas decarbonisation is highlighted as a priority in all three alternatives to business-as-usual growth, none of these pathways are discernibly aligned with Colombia's new NDC targets to 2030, nor ambitions to move towards carbon neutrality by 2050, as set forward in the MADS long-term strategy to face climate change. Specifically, fossil fuels remain a core component of all the energy scenarios, accounting for as much as 55% and 66% of energy supply across the pathways to 2050 (UPME, 2020[10]). Renewable energy plays an increasingly important role in lower-carbon inflection and disruption scenarios, but overall bioenergy use, despite large technical potential, does not change substantially across the scenarios. Moreover, "biofuels and residues", which include traditional use of biomass as well as modern forms of bioenergy and biofuels, are not broken down in the 2050 outlooks, and waste-to-energy is not included at all in the scenarios. Thus, while PEN messaging highlights certain fuels such as biogas both as a potential resource for electricity generation and as input to energy supply (e.g. as a natural gas substitute), there are no eventual targets provided under the scenarios.

Figure 2.2. PEN scenarios by fuel consumption, emissions and electricity capacity mix, 2019-50

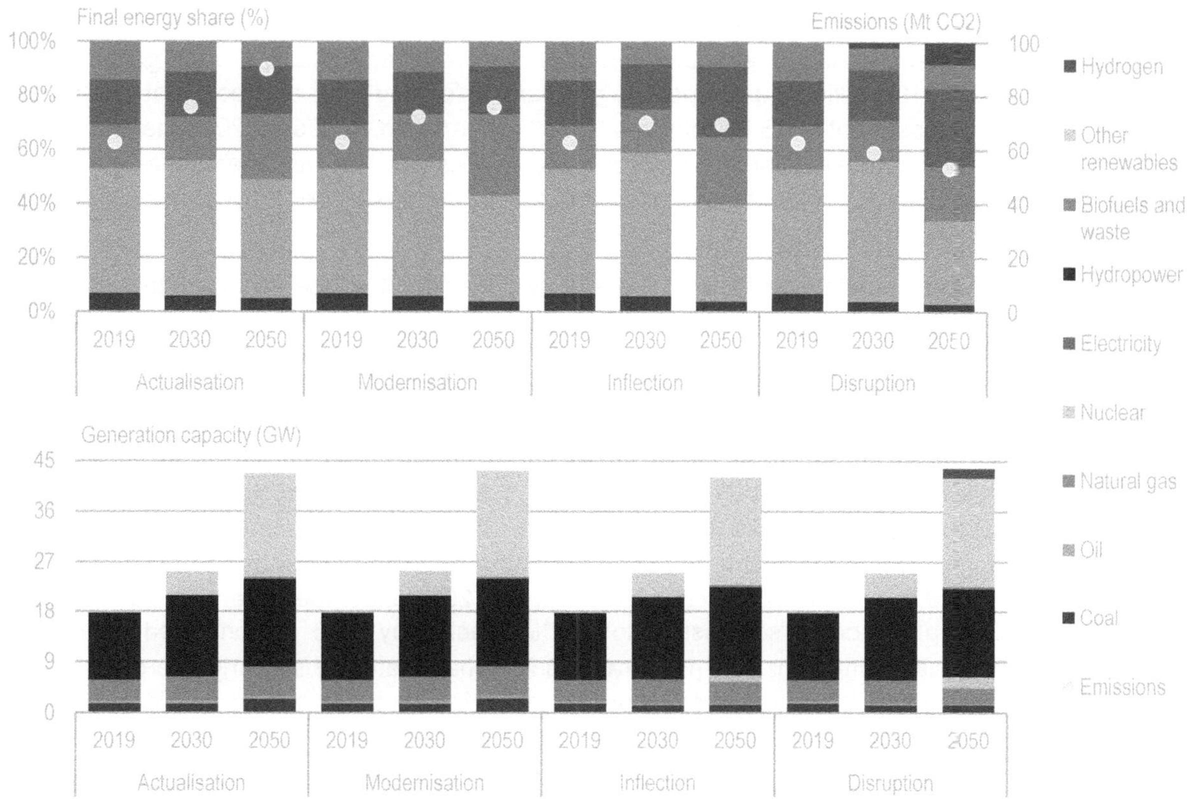


Source: adapted from (UPME, 2020[10]).

StatLink https://stat.link/d4vsgo

### *Bioenergy targets in the clean energy agenda will support project development*

A clearer energy transition strategy can provide targeted deployment levels to signal Colombia's intent to develop bioenergy solutions in line with its sustainable development objectives. This includes providing more specific decarbonisation targets for the overall energy sector, as these were not provided within the recently revised NDC. Rather, the update only provided high-level objectives to diversify the country's energy matrix, for instance by promoting self-generation of electricity through alternative fuel sources and by transforming electricity generation in ZNI. This leaves a large gap in expected details on what the energy mix would look like to achieve these objectives, including where solutions like bioenergy development would support the achievement of the country's clean energy transition.

Spelling out these fine points on how the government plans to achieve its NDC will send stronger signals on expectations and opportunities for clean energy development. UPME should consider development of an explicit NDC scenario, underscoring how Colombia can achieve its 51% emissions reduction targets by 2030 through specific clean energy technology deployment and with appropriate international support. This would send clearer indication on policy priorities and investment opportunities with respect to the government's intended medium- to long-term energy transition pathway. It also would help to clarify which of the PEN scenarios, or perhaps which elements within the different pathways, are expected to achieve the country's NDCs.

On-going preparation by DNP of a CONPES framework for the clean energy transition should help to provide a better assessment of these strategic energy policy priorities over the next decade and beyond. The overall CONPES process is an effective tool for defining, co-ordinating and leading policy actions across ministries, although its impact depends on the level of ambition and the specificity of actions outlined in this strategic framework. One relevant example is the action to promote investment in NCRE electricity generation projects under the 2018 Green Growth Policy. This required MME to provide guidance under its Decree No. 570 of 2018,[7] defining a competitive mechanism for long-term contracting of electric power generation projects. Subsequent MME Resolutions No. 40791[8] and No. 40795[9] of 2018 then provided the regulatory environment for power purchase agreements (PPAs) as well as operational guidance for renewable electricity auctions. Without these, renewable energy progress in recent years would likely have been considerably slower.

As DNP finalises its forthcoming CONPES on the energy transition, it will be important that subsequent measures spell out the planned targets and policy actions to decarbonise the energy sector. This includes clearly defining a long-term strategy to transition from fossil reliance towards solutions such as biogas and waste-to-energy technologies, as current signals do not provide sufficient foresight to clean energy project developers and potential investors. The CONPES could also recommend actions to set legally binding targets for the clean energy transition, as has been done in a growing number of countries. For example, Spain recently passed its Climate Change and Energy Transition Law (Ley de Cambio Climático y Transición Energética)[10] in May of 2021, setting forward a roadmap to reach carbon neutrality by 2050, with specific targets to double renewable energy penetration by 2030 (Climática, 2021[11]). The United Kingdom also enshrined its emissions reduction targets in May 2021 under the government's sixth Carbon Budget,[11] legally limiting the country's emissions to a 78% reduction by 2035, as compared to 1990 levels (Government of the United Kingdom, 2021[12]). France's National Assembly similarly approved a climate law[12] in 2021, not only establishing legal reductions for emissions but also setting specific measures to achieve those reductions, for instance by preventing future airport expansions (Reuters, 2021[13]).

### *Climate commitments are an opportunity to improve bioenergy capacity*

Colombia already has its own climate law (Ley No. 1931 of 2018)[13] that provides guidelines for the management of climate change, including the creation of a National System for Climate Change (Sistema Nacional de Cambio Climático) to formulate, co-ordinate, monitor and evaluate mitigation and adaptation policies. The 2018 Law also established a National Council on Climate Change (Consejo Nacional de Cambio Climático) to advise the Intersectoral Commission on Climate Change (Comisión Intersectorial de Cambio Climático, CICC) on decision-making in order to achieve an effective articulation and management of climate change measures. Additional precisions in the law included details on the economic and financial instruments that relevant public institutions should use in their mitigation and adaptation efforts.

The law and subsequent measures such as the 2020 CICC approval of the baseline to update Colombia's NDCs are laudable measures to empower climate action. Even so, specifics of how these ambitions will be achieved can be spelled out more assertively, providing a transparent long-term decarbonisation strategy to stimulate interest in deploying emissions abatement measures, including in non-energy sectors. For example, around 23% of the country's GHG emissZions are from agriculture, with another 31% from land-use change (e.g. deforestation). An additional 6.3% and 5.5% are from waste and industrial processes (ClimateWatch, 2021[1]). Bioenergy solutions can play a major role in abating these emissions and their environmental impact, for example through recovery of livestock manure for biogas production that would reduce both agricultural and energy-related GHG emissions (e.g. from industry and power generation), whilst equally avoiding soil degradation.

These opportunities, and subsequent actions to enable them, can be laid out further in the design of emerging policy measures such as Nationally Appropriate Mitigation Action (NAMA) that the government plans to implement in support of its NDC. Setting forth details on opportunities and policy ambitions for bioenergy development would equally complement wider socio-economic objectives, such as those set out in the country's 2018-22 National Development Plan (Plan Nacional de Desarrollo).[14] For example, the government is seeking support for NAMA preparation to develop renewable energy solutions in ZNI, where there are strong potential resources to improve electricity access and reliability through bioenergy solutions. Yet, the call[15] only notes clean fuels, solar and wind energy, whereas bioenergy technology and landfill gas collection are unchecked in the request for support (UNFCCC, 2021[-4]). A similar request seeking support for preparation of a Sustainable Bovine Livestock NAMA[16] looks to reduce emissions from enteric fermentation but does not note the opportunity to produce bioenergy as part of that NAMA (UNFCCC, 2021[15]). These are potentially missed opportunities to benefit from international support and expertise in the development of bioenergy solutions, for instance as secure, reliable and affordable electricity supply in ZNI.

The government is also considering formulation of a biogas NAMA, which would endeavour to align climate mitigation actions with use of biomass residuals for energy production (Government of Cololmbia, 2021[16]). The proposed NAMA can be an opportunity to outline strategic ambitions for bioenergy development, for example through production of biogas as a substitute for natural gas and LNG imports. It could equally consider relevant implementation support to achieve development of bioeconomy objectives and the 2020 National Strategy for the Circular Economy (Estrategia Nacional de Economía Circular),[17] for instance through technology solutions and best management practices for recovery of organic residues. Such considerations, including applying assessments like the Bioenergy and Food Security Approach,[18] would also help to ensure that development of bioenergy supply chains does not contribute to environmental degradation (e.g. competition for water resources or increased deforestation for biofuel crops).

These types of strategic considerations and subsequent policy signals will help to create the business case for bioenergy development and investment in these projects, building upon Colombia's impressive foundational framework that already distinguishes the opportunity for bioenergy solutions across a number of government strategies. For example, the 2016 National Policy for the Integral Management of Solid Waste (CONPES No. 3874)[19] set forth ambitions to reduce waste going to landfills by promoting the sorting, treatment, recycling and re-use of waste, including as recovery for energy production. Asserting the expected role bioenergy solutions will play in waste management and the clean energy transition will in turn help to make these opportunities clearer in a more predictable policy environment for market actors and investors. It will also help to identify where further policy action or market support is needed, for instance with respect to increasing landfill tipping fees or addressing barriers such as technology cost.

## Electricity planning can do more to facilitate bioenergy capacity additions

UPME's Reference Generation and Transmission Expansion Plan is the primary tool for electricity planning and development. It is expounded every three years with subsequent annual reviews. In the baseline scenario of the Plan, capacity additions take into account the existing pipeline of electricity projects that have been successfully approved by UPME for development, either through electricity auctions or by confirmation to connect to the grid. Remaining capacity needs with respect to expected future demand are then determined based on the cost of energy and foreseeable availability of generation technologies in UPME's project registry (specifically, those that have not yet been granted rights to connect to the grid). As such, previously approved projects play a critical role in the baseline electricity generation outlook. Technologies without a clear pipeline of projects accordingly are not well represented in UPME planning.

Colombia's large hydro development project, known as Ituango, is an additional, key determinant in the Reference Expansion Plan. There remains some uncertainty over whether Phase 2 of the Ituango project will be completed by 2034, thereby influencing the need for greater or lesser additional generation capacity. The uncertainty around this project (ranging from 1.2 to 2.4 GW) leaves considerable ambiguity for NCREs, where over 2.5 GW of renewable electricity generation would be cut if the Ituango project achieves its full capacity. In particular, the share of solar energy would drop from 3.8 to 2 GW of planned capacity. Wind would fall from 4.6 to 3.7 GW, and biomass would fall from 56 MW to 47 MW. Cogeneration likewise would shift modestly from 237 MW to 177 MW (Figure 2.3). By contrast, planned growth for coal and natural gas generation would remain unchanged.

**Figure 2.3. Variations in installed generation capacity under UPME's Expansion Plan, 2034**

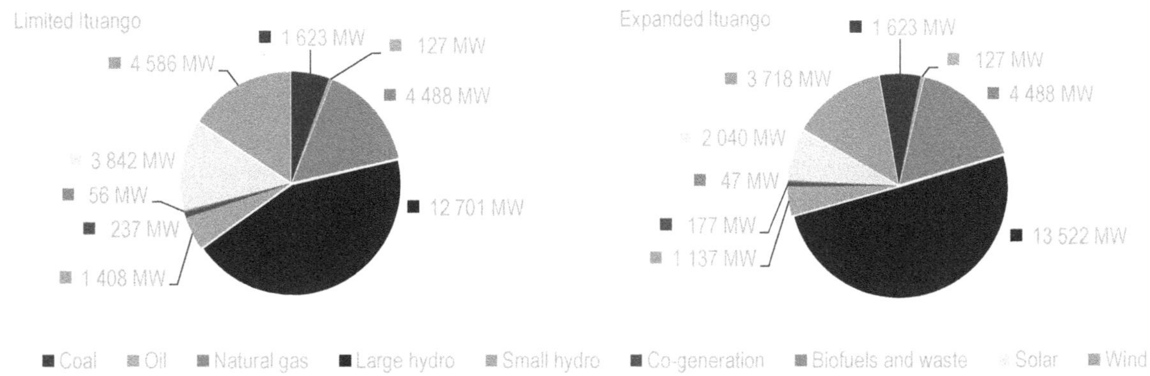


Source: adapted from (UPME, 2020[17]).

StatLink https://stat.link/pm6wkd

The current Reference Expansion Plan for 2020-34 has four additional scenarios that subsequently model: a one-year delay in the development of the Ituango project; greater influence of El Niño phenomena; inclusion of an emissions tax (USD 5 per tonne of $CO_2$); and the implementation of environmental flow[20] measures that would limit use of existing hydro capacity. These scenarios have negligible impact on the share of renewables, including bioenergy capacity additions, and underscore the critical influence of UPME's existing pipeline, project registry and grid connection requests on its electricity generation scenarios and Reference Expansion Plan.

While outlooks and scenarios based on current pipelines are not necessarily an issue for short-term projections, the reliance on these projects in the more medium-term UPME planning process does not particularly reflect the technical feasibility or overall socio-economic value of potential clean energy technologies like biomethane electricity production, including how these solutions can deliver on the government's clean energy and sustainable development ambitions.

### *Emphasis should focus on shaping a vision for clean, reliable and affordable electricity*

In other countries, electricity generation plans are often developed with respect to political targets, which either reflect upon or subsequently apply techno-economic models that consider how to meet power system needs in the most efficient or acceptable manner (Box 2.1). For example, Thailand's 2018-37 Power Development Plan explicitly targets renewable energy shares in electricity generation planning, sending a strong political and policy signal in line with the government's Alternative Energy Development Plan, National Strategy on Climate Change and its National Strategy for Eco-friendly Development and Growth (IEA, 2021[18]).

In Indonesia, the State Electricity Company, PLN, sets forth its ten-year Electricity Business Plan, reflecting priorities set forth in the National Electricity General Plan and the country's National Energy Policy, which provide an overarching policy framework with respect to the government's high-level strategy to achieve energy security and energy independence whilst addressing accessibility, affordability and sustainability of energy supply (OECD, 2021[19]).

### Box 2.1. Electricity development under the National Energy and Climate Plan of Greece

The European Union's 2018 Regulation on the Governance of the Energy Union and Climate Action required member states to outline their National Energy and Climate Plans to 2030. The objective of these plans was to provide a coherent picture of how countries aim to meet climate and energy objectives, giving greater visibility to how targets like renewable energy additions are expected to evolve over the next decade, whilst attracting investment and supporting job growth.

The government of Greece noted in its National Energy and Climate Plan that it plans to increase the share of renewable energy sources from 20% in 2020 to approximately 60% by 2030 (equivalent to 9 GW of new capacity over the period). This includes solar and wind additions as well as ambitions to increase bioenergy use for heating, cooling, transport and electricity generation. In particular, the country plans to quadruple the share of biomass and biogas in electricity generation to 1.6 TWh by 2030. It will do so by increasing installed generation capacity by over 200 MW over the next decade. To achieve this ambition, the Plan was accompanied by a number of planned policies and measures aimed at supporting investment, including use of feed-in-premiums, simplification of licencing procedures and prioritisation of energy from agricultural, industrial and municipal waste.

Greece's clean energy deployment targets were determined through a techno-economic assessment considering the potential of various renewable energy technologies to meet the country's energy demand over the next decade and beyond. This assessment was then used to inform market reforms and electricity planning to 2030. For instance, high shares of variable renewable energies like solar and wind will need to be integrated in the electricity system and will influence natural gas capacity additions, which are planned to provide system balancing and reserves as older lignite generation is phased out. Pumped hydro storage, hybrid hydro storage, battery storage and biogas capacity will also support reliable electricity supply. These capacity additions are subsequently featured in the Ten-Year Network Development Plan created by Greece's Independent Power Transmission Operator.

As such, Greece's National Energy and Climate Plan provides political commitment to increase the share of renewable energy as well as clear targets to inform energy system planning. These strategies allow for more targeted policy measures to achieve Greece's stated ambitions, including a clear sense of direction on capacity additions by technology type. In turn, these will help to drive project development and investment decisions for clean energy technologies like bioenergy solutions.

Source: (GoGreece, 2021[20]), (Hellenic Republic, 2019[21]) and (Trinomics, 2021[22]).

The National Electricity Plan of India similarly reflects high-level commitment to transform the electricity sector, specifically by retaining the government's target of deploying 275 GW of renewable energy by 2027. The plan also gives priority to electricity generation technologies (e.g. hydro, bioenergy and natural gas) that can help to deliver on related policy priorities such as the Indian government's goals on reducing air pollution and other GHGs (CEA, 2018[23]).

UPME should consider how best to reflect the role of clean energy technologies within the development of its Expansion Plan. For instance, it can take into account opportunities signalled in high-level policy ambitions such as the Bioeconomy and Circular Economy Strategies as part of the country's Reference Expansion Plan to 2034. Integrating these strategies into the country's electricity plans would also help to assess the future availability of sustainable bioenergy feedstock, for example by taking into account the influences of circular economy measures.

### *Facilitating planning and approval can help build up a pipeline of bioenergy projects*

UPME can also consider ways to facilitate the overall planning and approval process, which can disregard the impact of the lead times for projects to enter the pipeline in order to then be considered in the Expansion Plan, thereby creating a sort of recurring loop in which some technologies may consistently be under-represented. This is a particular consideration for bioenergy projects, which similar to other distributed renewable energy technologies may not have the experience or the capacity to navigate a multi-year approval process as would other large national or international project developers, for instance for utility-scale solar and wind developments.

Approval of capacity additions effectively happens in two stages (Figure 2.4). The first is listing in the generation project registry,[21] which indicates if a project has successfully undergone three years of feasibility studies and evaluation. This includes pre-feasibility assessment in Phase 1 (including environmental impact studies), a feasibility assessment considering technical and economic aspects in Phase 2, and finally verification of definitive designs and execution schedule in Phase 3. After successful listing, the second step is then allocation of grid capacity, which indicates that UPME has approved connection to supply electricity to the grid, depending on available capacity at the connection point. This agreement must be obtained in order for a project to be considered as confirmed in the Expansion Plan. Before going to construction, the project must also be accompanied by a bank guarantee, providing evidence that project development will ostensibly proceed.

Figure 2.4. Approval process for electricity generation projects and grid connection

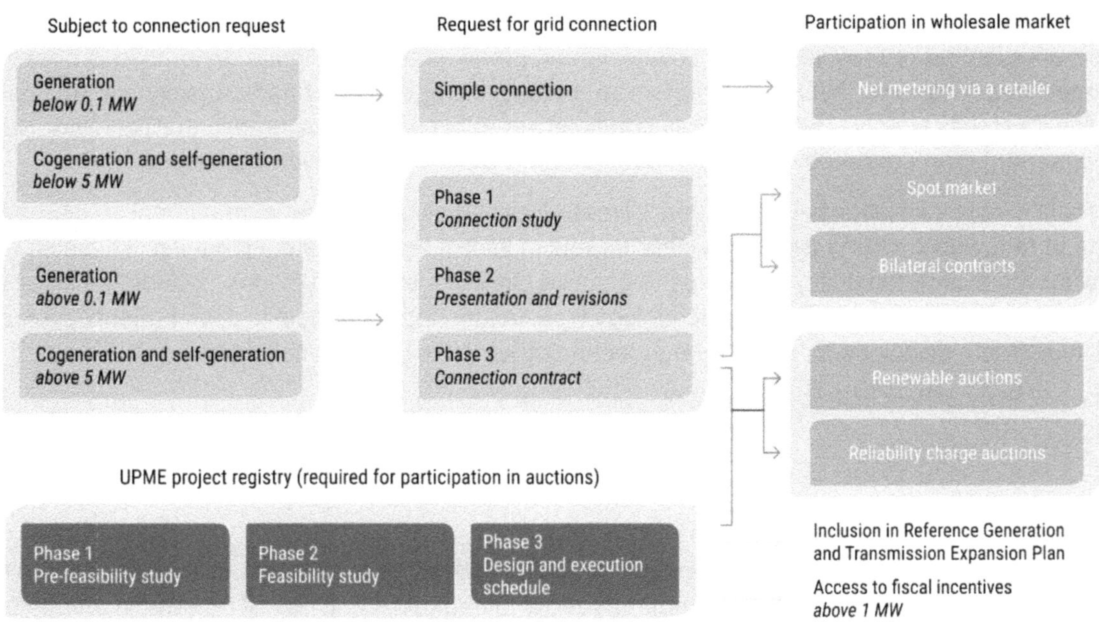


Source: adapted from (UPME, 2007[24]), (UPME, 2016[25]), (CREG, 1995[26]), (CREG, 1998[27]), and (CREG, 2006[28]).

This process can be a barrier, or at least cumbersome, for some project developers, such as bioenergy projects that may have to steer through a number of policy environments in order to demonstrate feasibility and obtain approvals, not only from respective authorities but also if requesting bank financing. The process can equally create bottlenecks within the pipeline, for example when failed or delayed projects already approved for connection hold up planned grid availability, consequently hindering new projects from obtaining grid connection rights (IRENA and USAID, 2021[29]). CREG published Resolution 233 of 2020[22] in response to this issue, establishing amongst other conditions a time limit for projects to connect to the grid. Yet, the Resolution did not address the potential front-end bottleneck for some projects simply to reach the approval process (and consequently be included in the Expansion Plan).

To facilitate greater interest and investment in bioenergy capacity development, government efforts can focus on supporting an initial pipeline of project approvals with the UPME registry For example, a pilot programme working with municipalities could work to create a pipeline of new biogas capacity additions. UPME could also consider running dedicated procurement for bioenergy projects, whereby considerations for the added benefits of those projects (e.g. locally available, round-the-clock power capacity without storage facilities) could be taken into account in generation and transmission expansion planning. These types of targeted measures would help to signal to project developers the interest in developing bioenergy capacity, whilst strengthening market demonstration of the economic potential for these technologies to potential investors (RVO, 2021[7]). They also would help to ensure future UPME planning reflects bioenergy opportunities as highlighted in broader strategic policy.

## References

CEA (2018), *National Electricity Plan: Volume I (Generation)*, Central Electricity Authority (CEA), Ministry of Power of the Government of India, https://policy.asiapacificenergy.org/sites/default/files/National%20Electricity%20Plan%20%28Volume%20I%29%20Generation.pdf (accessed on 24 September 2021). [23]

Chambers and Partners (2020), *Environmental Law 2020 - Colombia*, Environmental Law 2020, https://practiceguides.chambers.com/practice-guides/environmental-law-2020/colombia (accessed on 6 September 2021). [8]

Climate Action Tracker (2021), *Climate Target Update Tracker: Colombia*, https://climateactiontracker.org/climate-target-update-tracker/colombia/ (accessed on 21 September 2021). [2]

ClimateWatch (2021), *Historical Greenhouse Gas Emissions: Colombia*, https://www.climatewatchdata.org/ghg-emissions?chartType=area&end_year=2018&regions=COL&start_year=1990 (accessed on 16 September 2021). [1]

Climática (2021), *Definitively approved the first Climate Change Law in Spain (Aprobada la primera Ley de Cambio Climático de España)*, https://www.climatica.lamarea.com/aprobada-ley-de-cambio-climatico-espana/ (accessed on 23 September 2021). [11]

CREG (2006), *Resolución 106 de 2006*, Energy and Gas Regulatory Commission (Comisión de Regulación de Energía y Gas, CREG), http://apolo.creg.gov.co/Publicac.nsf/1c09d18d2d5ffb5b05256eee00709c02/217bfad39c5476fd0525785a007a6dab?OpenDocument (accessed on 5 October 2021). [28]

CREG (1998), *Resolución 70 de 1998*, Energy and Gas Regulatory Commission (Comisión de Regulación de Energía y Gas, CREG), http://apolo.creg.gov.co/Publicac.nsf/Indice01/Resoluci%C3%B3n-1998-CREG070-98 (accessed on 5 October 2021). [27]

CREG (1995), *Resolución 025 de 1995*, Energy and Gas Regulatory Commission (Comisión de Regulación de Energía y Gas, CREG), http://apolo.creg.gov.co/Publicac.nsf/Indice01/Resoluci%C3%B3n-1995-CRG95025 (accessed on 5 October 2021). [26]

DNP (2018), "CONPES 3934", in *Green Growth Policy (Política de Crecimiento Verde)*, National Council for Social and Economic Policy (Consejo Nacional de Política Económica y Social, CONPES), National Planning Department (Departamento Nacional de Planeación, DNP), https://colaboracion.dnp.gov.co/CDT/Conpes/Econ%C3%B3micos/3934.pdf (accessed on 6 September 2021). [6]

GoGreece (2021), *Market Reform Plan for Greece - Preliminary for consultation only-Subject to Revision*, Government of Greece, Athens. [20]

Government of Cololmbia (2021), *Consulting studies for the formulation of the biogas NAMA in Colombia (Estudios de Consultoría para la formulación del NAMA de biogás en Colombia)*, Government of Colombia. [16]

Government of Colombia (2020), *Bioeconomy for a lively and diverse Colombia: towards a knowledge-driven society (Bioeconomía para una Colombia potencia viva y diversa: hacia una sociedad impulsada por el conocimiento)*, https://minciencias.gov.co/sites/default/files/upload/paginas/bioeconomia_para_un_crecimiento_sostenible-gm_print.pdf (accessed on 22 September 2021). [9]

Government of Colombia (2015), *Intended Nationally Determined Contribution (Contribución Prevista Determinada a Nivel Nacional)*, https://www4.unfccc.int/sites/ndcstaging/PublishedDocuments/Colombia%20First/INDC%20Colombia.pdf (accessed on 21 September 2021). [3]

Government of the United Kingdom (2021), *UK enshrines new target in law to slash emissions by 78% by 2035*, https://www.gov.uk/government/news/uk-enshrines-new-target-in-law-to-slash-emissions-by-78-by-2035 (accessed on 22 September 2021). [12]

Hellenic Republic (2019), *National Energy and Climate Plan*, Ministry of Environment and Energy, Athens. [21]

IEA (2021), *The Potential Role of Carbon Pricing in Thailand's Power Sector*, International Energy Agency (IEA), Paris, https://www.iea.org/reports/the-potential-role-of-carbon-pricing-in-thailands-power-sector (accessed on 29 September 2021). [18]

IRENA and USAID (2021), *Renewable energy auctions in Colombia: context, design and results*, International Renewable Energy Agency (IRENA) and United States Agency for International Development (USAID), https://www.irena.org/publications/2021/March/Renewable-energy-auctions-in-Colombia. [29]

MADS (2020), *Colombia presented its long-term strategy to face climate change by 2050 (Colombia presentó su Estrategia de largo plazo para hacer frente al cambio climático al 2050)*, Ministry of Environment and Sustainable Development (Ministerio de Ambiente y Desarrollo Sostenible, MADS), https://www.minambiente.gov.co/index.php/noticias/4739-colombia-presento-su-estrategia-de-largo-plazo-para-hacer-frente-al-cambio-climatico-al-2050 (accessed on 21 September 2021). [4]

OECD (2021), *Clean Energy Finance and Investment Mobilisation: Colombia*, Organisation for Economic Co-operation and Development (OECD), https://www.oecd.org/cefim/colombia/ (accessed on 4 October 2021). [5]

OECD (2021), *Clean Energy Finance and Investment Policy Review of Indonesia*, Green Finance and Investment, OECD Publishing, Paris, https://dx.doi.org/10.1787/0007dd9d-en. [19]

Reuters (2021), *French parliament approves climate change bill to green the economy*, https://www.reuters.com/world/europe/french-parliament-approves-wide-ranging-climate-change-bill-green-economy-2021-05-04/ (accessed on 22 September 2021). [13]

RVO (2021), *Waste Management in the LATAM Region: Business Opportunities for the Netherlands in waste/circular economy sector in eight countries of Latin America*, The Netherlands Enterprise Agency (RVO), https://www.rvo.nl/sites/default/files/2021/02/Report_LATAM_Waste_Management_feb_2021.pdf (accessed on 16 September 2021). [7]

Trinomics (2021), *Analysis on biomass in National Energy and Climate Plans*, Trinomics, Rotterdam. [22]

UNFCCC (2021), *NS-222 - Energy with Renewable Sources in non-interconnected areas*, NAMA Seeking Support for Preparation, United Nations Framework Convention on Climate Change (UNFCCC), https://www4.unfccc.int/sites/PublicNAMA/_layouts/un/fccc/nama/NamaSeekingSupportForPreparation.aspx?ID=147&viewOnly=1 (accessed on 22 September 2021). [14]

UNFCCC (2021), *NS-225 - Sustainable Bovine Livestock*, NAMA Seeking Support for Preparation, United Nations Framework Convention on Climate Change (UNFCCC), https://www4.unfccc.int/sites/PublicNAMA/_layouts/un/fccc/nama/NamaSeekingSupportForPreparation.aspx?ID=150&viewOnly=1 (accessed on 23 September 2021). [15]

UPME (2020), *Generation and Transmission Reference Expansion Plan 2020-2034 (Plan de expansión de referencia generación – transmisión 2020-2034)*, Planning Unit of the Ministry of Mines and Energy (Unidad de Planeación Minero Energética, UPME), http://www.siel.gov.co/Inicio/Generaci%c3%b3n/PlanesdeExpansi%c3%b3nGeneraci%c3%b3nTransmisi%c3%b3n/tabid/111/Default.aspx (accessed on 17 September 2021). [17]

UPME (2020), *National Energy Plan 2020-2050 (Plan Energético Nacional 2020-2050)*, Planning Unit of the Ministry of Mines and Energy (Unidad de Planeación Minero Energética, UPME), http://www1.upme.gov.co/DemandayEficiencia/Documents/PEN_2020_2050/Plan_Energetico_Nacional_2020_2050.pdf (accessed on 17 September 2021). [10]

UPME (2016), *Resolución 143 de 2016*, Planning Unit of the Ministry of Mines and Energy (Unidad de Planeación Minero Energética, UPME), http://www.siel.gov.co/siel/documentos/documentacion/Generacion/143_2016.pdf (accessed on 5 October 2021). [25]

UPME (2007), *Resolución 638 de 2007*, Planning Unit of the Ministry of Mines and Energy (Unidad de Planeación Minero Energética, UPME), http://www.suin-juriscol.gov.co/viewDocument.asp?ruta=Resolucion/4048051 (accessed on 5 October 2021). [24]

## Notes

[1] For more information (in Spanish), see: https://www.dnp.gov.co/Crecimiento-Verde/Paginas/Politica-crecimiento-verde.aspx.

[2] For more information (in Spanish), see: https://www.minambiente.gov.co/index.php/estrategia-nacional-de-economia-circular-ec.

[3] For more information (in Spanish), see: https://www.minambiente.gov.co/index.php/component/content/article/28-plantilla-asuntos-ambientales-y-sectorial-y-urbana.

[4] For more information (in Spanish), see: https://minciencias.gov.co/sites/default/files/upload/paginas/bioeconomia_para_un_crecimiento_sostenible-qm_print.pdf.

[5] More information on actions and experiences to promote the development of bioenergy solutions in Latin America and the Caribbean can be found in the LEDS-LAC Bioenergy Community of Practice: https://ledslac.org/comunidades-de-practica/bioenergy/.

[6] For more information, see: https://www.ocio.usda.gov/sites/default/files/docs/2012/SM%201044-010%20Establishment%20of%20the%20USDA%20Bioeconomy%20Council%20and%20the%20Bioeconomy%20Council%20Coordination%20Committee.htm.

[7] For more information (in Spanish), see: http://es.presidencia.gov.co/normativa/normativa/DECRETO%200570%20DEL%2023%20DE%20MARZO%20DE%202018.pdf.

[8] For more information (in Spanish), see: https://www.minenergia.gov.co/documents/10192/24067478/081118_Modifica+la+Resoluci%C3%B3n+4+0791+de+2018_231118.pdf/65a03d4c-ac19-459b-89f0-76599d3e6655.

[9] For more information (in Spanish), see: https://jurinfo.jep.gov.co/normograma/compilacion/docs/resolucion_minminas_40795_2018.htm.

[10] For more information (in Spanish), see: https://www.boe.es/diario_boe/txt.php?id=BOE-A-2021-8447.

[11] For more information, see: https://www.theccc.org.uk/publication/sixth-carbon-budget/.

[12] For more information (in French), see: https://www.vie-publique.fr/loi/278460-loi-22-aout-2021-climat-et-resilience-convention-citoyenne-climat#:~:text=La%20loi%20%22Climat%20et%20R%C3%A9silience,un%20esprit%20de%20justice%20sociale.

[13] For more information (in Spanish), see: https://www.minambiente.gov.co/images/cambioclimatico/pdf/LEY_1931_DEL_27_DE_JULIO_DE_2018_LEY_DE_CAMBIO_CLIM%C3%81TICO.pdf.

[14] For more information (in Spanish), see: https://www.dnp.gov.co/DNPN/Paginas/Plan-Nacional-de-Desarrollo.aspx.

[15] For more information, see: https://www4.unfccc.int/sites/PublicNAMA/_layouts/un/fccc/nama/NamaSeekingSupportForPreparation.aspx?ID=147&viewOnly=1.

[16] For more information, see: https://www4.unfccc.int/sites/PublicNAMA/_layouts/un/fccc/nama/NamaSeekingSupportForPreparation.aspx?ID=150&viewOnly=1.

[17] For more information (in Spanish), see: http://www.andi.com.co/Uploads/Estrategia%20Nacional%20de%20EconA%CC%83%C2%B3mia%20Circular-2019%20Final.pdf_637176135049017259.pdf.

[18] For more information on the United Nations Food and Agricultural Organisation (FAO) Bioenergy and Food Security (BEFS) Approach, see: https://www.fao.org/energy/bioenergy/bioenergy-and-food-security/en/.

[19] For more information (in Spanish), see: https://colaboracion.dnp.gov.co/CDT/Conpes/Econ%C3%B3micos/3874.pdf.

[20] Environmental flows (caudal ambiental) are the precise flows, timing and quality of water to maintain water ecosystems.

[21] For more information (in Spanish), see: http://www.siel.gov.co/Inicio/Generaci%C3%B3n/Inscripci%C3%B3ndeproyectosdeGeneraci%C3%B3n/tabid/113/Default.aspx.

[22] For more information (in Spanish), see: http://apolo.creg.gov.co/Publicac.nsf/1c09d18d2d5ffb5b05256eee00709c02/58da78f1ed25d4fd0525864e006f6057/$FILE/Creg233-2020.pdf.

# 3 Regulatory measures to improve the case for sustainable bioenergy

Policy reforms and market incentives played a critical role in enabling early growth of bioenergy cogeneration in the sugar and palm industries in Colombia. Over the last decade, the country's regulatory framework for renewable energy has provided further clarity on the operational rules and remuneration for clean energy additions, such as bioenergy self-generation. Improving the transparency on grid-access rules and connection costs, whilst aligning incentives to encourage retailers to procure distributed energy generation, can further increase opportunities for bioenergy development. Strengthening the regulatory framework on waste management, for instance, to address low landfill and waste collection fees, will also improve incentives for bioenergy projects. Additional regulatory signals could include use of emissions trading and carbon pricing mechanisms to drive demand for clean energy sources like biogas for industry use.

## Highlights

- Market incentives and policy measures over the last two decades encouraged early growth in bioenergy capacity additions like cogeneration in Colombia's sugar and palm industries. Lessons from these developments, including important regulatory reforms that supported the business case for industry investment, can be applied to encourage bioenergy opportunities in other industries, such as dairy production and hog farming.
- Legal measures like the Renewable Energy Law of 2014 have played a critical role in establishing the operational rules and remuneration for renewable energy projects, but there remain barriers for bioenergy projects. The regulatory framework can do more to provide transparent criteria on grid-access rules and connection costs, including clear guidance on negotiations for back-up supply charges, whose cost calculations are not readily understood.
- Current renewable portfolio standards do not give credit to retailers for renewable energy production used on-site by regulated consumers, nor for renewable electricity sold to unregulated customers, which represent about half of Colombia's electricity demand. Addressing these restrictions would provide greater inventive for retailers to secure potential clean energy agreements, including through bioenergy capacity additions.
- Colombia can learn from international experiences with renewable energy certificates and other policy tools that have encouraged sourcing of renewable energy. This can include use of financial incentives and support for bioenergy projects, alongside obligations for industry and/or large energy consumers to increase their share of clean energy consumption.
- Landfill and waste collection fees are typically low in Colombia, and waste management companies and landfill operators have little incentive to sort and recover waste as fees apply to the amount of waste collected or disposed of. Firm targets and/or mandatory retrieval of certain wastes, paired with progressive increases in the overall value of fees and landfill taxes, will encourage greater sorting and treatment of waste, including for waste-to-energy applications.

Colombia's energy policy environment has continued to transform since the 1990s, when severe energy insufficiency and power outages driven by an el Niño event led to the energy crisis of 1992. This resulted in critical reforms such as the passage of Law 142 of 1994 (and modification under Law 689 of 2001) that established a number of core public services, regulatory commissions, market competition rules and standards (Table 3.1). Concerns over the reliability of electricity supply also led to the development of a wholesale electricity market (Mercado de Energía Mayorista). Since then, policy reforms have continued to promote development of a reliable and affordable energy system, including the passage of regulations aimed at renewable energy, such as Law 697 of 2001,[1] which targeted the "rational and efficient use of energy and the use of other non-conventional energy sources".

These actions, complemented by measures such as tax reform for renewable energy projects, have helped to foster clean energy growth over the last two decades, including early bioenergy developments in the sugar and palm industries. Strengthening this regulatory framework, for example through targeted policy to realise ambitions in the forthcoming bioeconomy Nationally Appropriation Mitigation Action, will further facilitate development of bioenergy solutions, ensuring that regulations address any remaining policy gaps and market barriers to these opportunities. This includes ensuring the regulatory environment clearly addresses the role of waste management and related market incentives for its recovery for energy production. Colombia already has a strong policy regime for waste collection and disposal, and this, too, can be expounded to realise bioenergy opportunities whilst achieving the country's circular economy and bioeconomy ambitions.

Table 3.1. Highlights of electricity market regulations since the 1992 energy crisis

| |
|---|
| **Law 142 of 1994** (later modified by Law 689 of 2001) established the regime of domestic public services, fixing rules and principles of economic competition |
| **Law 143 of 1994** established the regime for generation, interconnection, transmission, distribution and marketing of electricity |
| **CREG Resolution 055 of 1994** regulated activities of electricity generation in the National Interconnected System |
| **CREG Resolution 024 and 025 of 1995** regulated the commercial aspects of the wholesale energy market and establishing the network code as part of the operating regulations in the National Interconnected System |
| **CREG Resolution 020 of 1996** established rules to promote free competition in the wholesale electricity market |
| **GREG Resolution 034 of 2001** issued rules on the operation of the wholesale electricity market |
| **CREG Resolution 071 of 2006** issued the remuneration methodology for the reliability charge |
| **CREG Resolution 091 of 2007** established the general methodologies to remunerate the activities of generation, distribution, and retail of electric energy in Non-Interconnected Zones |
| **CREG Resolution 051 of 2009** modified the price scheme, ideal dispatch and rule determining the price of the wholesale market exchange |
| **CREG Resolution 156 of 2011** established regulation on the retail of public electricity service |

## Early bioenergy cogeneration stresses the importance of a clear regulatory framework

Bioenergy cogeneration in Colombia's sugar and palm industries started in the late 1990s, when early adoptions began making use of abundant sugarcane bagasse and palm oil residues to provide combined heat and power in those industries. The legal framework allowing for this cogeneration was defined notably under Energy and Gas Regulation Commission (Comisión de Regulación de Energía y Gas, CREG) Resolutions 85 and 86 of 1996[2] and subsequent CREG Resolution 107 of 1998.[3] These determined the regulatory norms for cogeneration and set the legal conditions for co-production of thermal and electric energy as an integral part of an industry process (CCC, 2016[1]). The regulations also set forward the rules for access to the grid for these projects.

Law 788 of 2002[4] later established a tax exemption over 15 years for income generated from the sale of electricity from wind, agricultural waste and bioenergy sources. Eligible projects, including in theory cogeneration, qualified for the incentive as long as they obtained emissions trading certificates, in accordance with the terms of the Kyoto Protocol, and reinvested at least 50% of the revenues from the sale of those permits in social projects situated within the area served by the utility. In principle, these should have encouraged some further bioenergy development but, in practice, the number of such projects remained limited, where electricity sales from cogeneration essentially remained constant through the 2000s.

Law 1215 of 2008[5] and ensuing CREG Resolution 5 of 2010[6] marked a clear turning point in this lack of progress by legally differentiating cogeneration from other forms of energy production. Specifically, these regulations provided technical requirements and incentives for cogeneration, including exemptions for payment of contributions on energy destined for self-consumption. Law 1215 also opened the door to bilateral contracts (either with the retailer or with unregulated commercial customers) for co-generators that ensure guaranteed power over 20 MW. This re-invigorated industry appetite for combined heat and electricity production, resulting in a sizeable jump of new cogeneration capacity and resultant electricity sales to the grid after 2009 (Figure 3.1). Additional policy measures such as tax incentives provided under the 2010 Programme for the Rational and Efficient Use of Energy and other non-conventional renewable energy (PROURE)[7] and the landmark 2014 Renewable Energy Law further encouraged use of cogeneration with bioenergy and other renewable energy sources. By 2020, cogeneration capacity supplied to the grid, still mostly from the sugar and palm industries, reached 723 GWh of electricity, with a further 989 GWh of energy that were self-consumed by industry itself (Asocaña, 2021[2]).

**Figure 3.1. Evolution of electricity sales from grid connected cogeneration, 1998-2021**

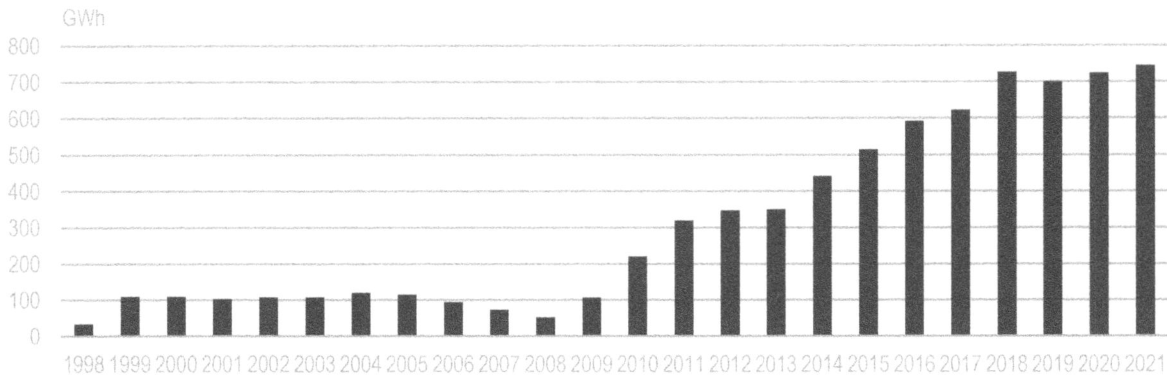


Note: GWh = Gigawatt hour. 2021 data is from January to September.
Source: adapted from (CCC, 2016[1]), (Asocaña, 2021[2]) and (XM, 2021[3]).

StatLink https://stat.link/whqv8l

Other reforms provided additional incentives to develop bioenergy cogeneration capacity in industry. For example, regulatory changes in the late 2000s enabled cogeneration plants to sell surplus electricity to the wholesale market, but they did not allow these plants to participate in reliability charge auctions for firm power. To address this limitation and improve the business case for eventual cogeneration opportunities, CREG Resolution 153 of 2013[8] enabled co-generators using bioenergy to obtain supply contracts for "fuel of agricultural origin" (Combustible de Origen Agrícola), receiving a reliability charge so long as they obtained guarantees through a technical report on the availability of fuel over the contracted period. This proved particularly effective for the sugar and palm cogeneration (e.g. in centrally dispatched sugar mills) that were able to meet the fuel requirements given their strong supply of feedstock (Asocaña, 2014[4]).

These regulatory reforms and market incentives have encouraged considerable growth in bioenergy co-generation over the last decade by creating the legal framework for those operations and importantly by supporting the clear business case for industry investment in cogeneration capacity. In fact, the Colombian Sugarcane Growers Association (Asociación de Cultivadores de Caña de Azúcar, Asocaña) consistently highlights the value of cogeneration in its annual association reports. It also works with the industry to bring forward regulatory weaknesses that may impede future capacity additions. For example, challenges such as penalties for reactive power[9] havehighlighted a potentially disruptive cost, even if new investments in the sugarcane industry are still proceeding. Other challenges include costs related to grid connections (e.g. possible need for investment in substations) and difficulties accessing finance (e.g. to upgrade to more efficient boilers) for some actors (see Chapter 4).

Lessons from the cogeneration market, particularly around creating a clear legal and business environment for generator participation, can be applied to the development of prospective bioenergy opportunities in other industries such as dairy production and hog farming, where the attractiveness of bioenergy solutions may be less obvious or where the regulatory environment may make the business case for recovery of waste in energy production challenging (e.g. in procuring waste streams).

## Clarifying the regulatory environment for bioenergy will support greater project development

The Renewable Energy Law of 2014 was a major milestone for clean energy projects in Colombia, setting the framework for their use and adopting regulations for their integration in the market. A number of decrees and resolutions have successively strengthened this regulatory framework for renewable energy, including its use in electricity generation (Table 3.2).

For example, Planning Unit of the Ministry of Mines and Energy (Unidad de Planeación Minero Energética, UPME) Resolution 45 of 2016 created the context for net metering and allowed self-generators and distributed electricity generation to connect to the grid. CREG Resolutions 15 and 30 of 2018[10] then established the operational rules and remuneration for those projects, and MME Decree 570,[11] including subsequent MME Resolutions No. 40791 and No. 40795 of 2018, established the design for 15-year power purchase agreement (PPAs), with additional guidance on renewable energy auctions. Most recently, Law 2099 of 2021[12] set forth provisions to modernise legislation for the energy transition and to stimulate the development of non-conventional renewable energy (NCRE), including new definitions for green hydrogen (from renewable energy sources) and blue hydrogen (using carbon capture and storage) as NCRE.

These reforms have supported a growing share of renewables in Colombia's energy mix, including from recent solar and wind additions. The evolving regulatory framework has also supported development of bioenergy technologies, even if there remain some barriers to enable greater development of those solutions. For example, the Renewable Energy Law (Law 1715 of 2014) prioritised the use of local renewable energy resources, thereby indirectly promoting nearby agricultural, industrial and municipal waste for recovery in energy production. The Law also legally defined these potential energy sources from organic materials ("biomasa") and from energy recovered from solid waste as bioenergy.

Definitions and regulatory norms for bioenergy were also elaborated in policies such as CREG Resolution 240 of 2016,[13] which created the regulatory conditions for development of biogas and biomethane capacity. Importantly, these measures reinforced bioenergy as eligible for NCRE incentives, such as those under Presidential Decree 2143 of 2015,[14] which provided a 50% income tax reduction over a five-year period with rules on accelerated depreciation. The Decree also provided value-added tax and import duty exemptions on purchase of goods and services for the production and use of energy from NCRE. Decree 829 of 2020[15] by the Ministry of Finance and Public Credit (Ministerio de Hacienda y Crédito Público) then streamlined the process for evaluating project eligibility in order to reduce administrative procedures for securing such fiscal incentives. Specifically, the decree made UPME the sole responsible entity for the process, effectively halving approval time from three months to 45 days (Sanchez Molina, 2020[5]).

Access to such incentives has been particularly important for bioenergy development, where these technologies would likely struggle to be financially viable without such fiscal incentives, especially for early adopters (Alzate-Arias et al., 2018[6]). Specifically, regulation governing application and remuneration of bioenergy capacity is critical to project development. This is evidenced by growth in electricity sold to the grid from bioenergy cogeneration in the sugarcane and palm oil industries, where a clear, legal revenue stream helped to justify investments in expanded capacity and improved generation efficiency to maximise recovery of waste residues (RVO, 2021[7]).

Table 3.2. Highlights of legal measures targeting renewable energy development

| |
|---|
| Congressional **Law 788 of 2002** regulated the sale of electricity from wind energy, biomass and agricultural waste, exempting these from income tax for 15 years under certain conditions. |
| **MME Resolution No. 18-0919 of 2010** adopted the 2010-15 Action Plan to develop PROURE, including defining the objectives, sub-programmes and provisions adopted in that regard. The validity of the plan was extended until June 2016, when the 2016-20 Plan was adopted. |
| **Law 1715 of 2014** (the Renewable Energy Law) that regulated the integration of NCRE in the national energy system, with measures for 50% income tax reduction, a value-added tax exemption, import duty exemption and accelerated depreciation rules (under Decree 2143/2015). The Law also created a fund for non-conventional energy and efficient energy management (Fondo de Energías No Convencionales y Gestión Eficiente de la Energía, FENOGE) and increased the electricity tariff by 0.01 USD/kWh to subsidise the fund. |
| **UPME Resolution 281 of 2015** defined the maximum power limit of small-scale self-generation and included VAT exemptions on machinery, equipment and labour costs for non-hydro renewable energy projects. Import tariffs were exempted on machinery, equipment and materials, alongside rules for a boosted depreciation rate up to 20% per year. The Resolution also expanded the income tax deduction for non-hydro renewables, from five to 15 years, and thus the rate to 150%. |
| **UPME Resolution 45 of 2016** set to ease the process of grid-connections for power plants and established net-metering regulations for generation up to 100 kilowatt (peak) to sell surplus electricity. |
| **MME Decree 570 of 2018** established the blueprints for long-term PPAs through renewable energy auctions. MME Resolutions 40791 and 40795 of 2018 then provided operational guidance for the auctions. |
| **CREG Resolution 30 of 2018** set the operational and commercial rules for the integration of self-generation and distributed generation (below 100 kilowatts, between 100 kilowatts and 1 MW, and between 1 and 5 MW) and **CREG Resolution 15 of 2018** set the methodology for the remuneration and back-up supply of electricity in the national grid. |
| **MME Resolution 49715 of 2019** mandated distributors to procure at least 10% of energy sold to regulated customers from solar, biomass, micro-hydro, wind or tidal power. |
| Congressional **Law 1955 of 2019** modified Law 1715 to increase the benefits of income tax reduction for NCRE generators from five to 15 years. It also added codes for custom tariff reductions on the import of solar panels and other items related to renewable energy generation. |
| **Ministry of Finance and Public Credit Decree 829 of 2020** regulated granting of tax-related incentives for NCRE generation. It also stated that UPME shall be the only authority in charge of evaluating these benefits and their application. |
| **Law 2036 of 2020** authorised the national government to finance support, using contributions from the General Budget of the Nation and the General System of Royalties, for the participation of territorial entities in the generation, distribution, retail and self-generation projects for small-scale and distributed generation with NCRE. |
| **Law 2099 of 2021** modified the regulatory framework for NCRE and legally established green and blue hydrogen as NCRE. Tax exemptions were extended to power storage, smart metering systems and power management, as well as for investments relating to green and blue hydrogen. The law also established provisions on the energy transition, revitalisation of the energy market and economic recovery. |

For other bioenergy applications, the business model can be less certain, although Law 2036 of 2020,[16] which recently authorised territorial entities to participate in NCRE development by making use of national funds, should help, as it included specific references to bioenergy and waste-to-energy projects. Still, there remain other critical barriers to widespread bioenergy project development. For example, uncertainty around current regulation for the sale of biogas (e.g. for self-generators connecting to the grid) only serves to compound lack of capacity and experience with such technologies in Colombia. The processes for obtaining licences, incentives and permits for biogas projects can also be complicated and lengthy, and delays in connection of new biogas projects to the grid have been highlighted as an issue (Duarte, Loaiza and Majano, 2021[8]). Part of this is due to the discretionary nature of connection rules, where the regulatory framework can do more to provide transparent criteria for accepted requests. Technical standards and regulations can also be poorly understood by relevant actors, especially in the agricultural sector where there is large untapped potential for biogas development but which has little to no experience in the management and commercialisation of power generation.

### *Connection rules and procedures can do more to facilitate bioenergy capacity*

Addressing these barriers, for instance through clearer guidance on grid-access regulation, will help to encourage new additions in distributed and self-generation bioenergy technologies. UPME could also expand its connection assessment to take into account the potential role of biogas projects in demand response, for example looking at how these projects could partake in the Voluntary Disconnectable Demand Programme (El Programa de Demanda Desconectable Voluntaria). This programme provides the opportunity for self-generation to respond during peak demand periods or when electricity prices are high, either by reducing demand or by making additional power generation available to the electricity system.

The regulatory environment can likewise do more to target policy for bioenergy connections. For example, the legal framework for distributed generation and self-generators to sell surplus electricity to the grid was established under UPME Resolutions 281 of 2015[17] and 45 of 2016.[18] Yet, only small amount of solar (0.6 MW) and biogas (2.2 MW) self-generation capacity was approved for connection as of 2018. The latter was a biogas installation in Cundinamarca supported by grants from the German investment bank, kFW, to use wastewater from the local dairy food industry for cogeneration.

Part of this limited pipeline of additions was due to competition with fossil fuel generation, which also benefited for connection and as of 2018 made up more than 85% of grid-connected distributed and self- generation (UPME, 2021[9]). Subsequent guidance on operational and commercial rules for net metering (passed under CREG Resolutions 15 and 30 of 2018[19]) aimed to enable greater NCRE connection, although this had a more visible impact on solar connections, which reached 34 MW of capacity approved for connection to the grid by 2021. By contrast, approved bioenergy capacity only increased to around 2.9 MW by mid-2021, and the new additions (a 0.2 MW bagasse project and a 0.4 MW agricultural waste project) are still pending connection. Three additional bioenergy projects using agricultural residue are under review, but they would only add around 1.6 MW of new capacity.

This low interest in new connections is partially due to requirements for back-up power supply contracts for systems above 100 kilowatts (under CREG Resolution 15 of 2018), which in addition to reactive energy payments (for any generators that do not have automatic voltage control), have been highlighted as an important cost consideration for distributed energy projects, including bioenergy (Morganstein et al., 2021[10]). Additionally, negotiations on back-up supply charges can be challenging to navigate, and their cost calculations are complicated and not readily understood. This can limit interest in developing bioenergy solutions, and in some instances it has likely encouraged certain players to install smaller, on-site solar systems, even if larger installations or use of bioenergy technologies would offset a greater share of their energy consumption. UPME's record of requests for connection to the grid also highlights a clear challenge for bioenergy additions, where over 2.7 MW of said projects were rejected for connection since

2018, including five industrial projects using agricultural residues and two proposed livestock projects (UPME, 2021[9]).

## *Renewable portfolio targets can work with bioenergy projects, rather than against them*

Recent regulatory reforms have since aimed to strengthen the opportunity for renewable energy projects, but again, these have not necessarily addressed opportunities for bioenergy connections. For example, MME Resolution 49715 of 2019[20] mandated that at least 10% of electricity sold to regulated customers by retailers be sourced from NCRE (excluding all hydro) through long-term contracts of ten years or more. Monitoring of these requirements will commence in 2023, where the recent renewable energy auctions helped retailers to begin securing their requirements through the new solar and wind capacity additions. The mandates also helped to enable the successful auctions, as retailers were looking to secure certain amounts of renewable energy capacity.

Yet, the specific rules for the renewable portfolio requirements do not readily encourage or facilitate retailers in securing bioenergy capacity (amongst other potential renewable opportunities). Specifically, the 10% mandate does not give credit to retailers for any renewable energy production used on-site by their regulated[21] consumers (e.g. rooftop solar or on-site biogas). Moreover, the quota rules do not allow retailer credits for renewable electricity sold to unregulated customers, which represent about half of electricity demand (Morganstein et al., 2021[10]). Without such credits, the requirements provide little incentive for retailers to pursue or facilitate potential clean energy agreements (e.g. via off-site PPAs) with unregulated commercial and industrial users, whose interest in procuring clean electricity, for instance through renewable energy certificate (REC) purchases, continues to grow (CEIA, 2019[11]). The portfolio standard rules also do not incentivise seeking agreements with potential self-generators or co-generators who could use their production capacity (e.g. from biogas co-processing) to sell surplus electricity (e.g. through bundled or unbundles RECs).

Colombia already has a few such REC initiatives, for example under the International Renewable Energy Certification standard, although it does not have an official REC system or regulations regarding the issuance of RECs. In late 2020, the grid and wholesale electricity market operator, XM, launched a REC registry and tracking system ("EcoGox"), which should help to provide improved transparency and accountability for this market to grow (Morganstein et al., 2021[10]). Still, formal guidance and/or measures to link RECs to the regulatory framework (e.g. tying RECs to carbon reduction credits under Decree 926 of 2017[22] and the expected development of an emissions trading scheme (IETA, 2021[12]) would support wider market participation. This includes improved linkages to the portfolio requirements under Resolution 49715, whereby retailers would be more motivated to engage consumers in clean electricity development and REC exchanges if these counted towards renewable portfolio targets. Improved incentive for retailers to work actively with consumers to procure clean electricity would also support the business case to develop bioenergy projects (with added economic benefit from RECs trading).

Colombia can also learn from international experience with RECs and other models for corporate sourcing of renewables (e.g. PPAs through power wheeling arrangements). This includes possible targeting of bioenergy development through these agreements or through an explicit REC framework. For example, the Renewables Obligation Certificates scheme in the United Kingdom awarded more certificates per MWh produced for offshore wind projects, given their more complex nature (e.g. structural design, capex and maintenance costs) compared to other renewable energy sources. Specifically, the number of certificates awarded varied according to the technology, where offshore wind generation received twice as many certificates per MWh than other renewable energy technologies between 2012 and 2014 and 1.5 times as many certificates in 2014 and 2015 (Riley and Zarnowiecki, 2012[13]).

MME and CREG can similarly consider ways to co-ordinate policy and regulatory frameworks to create a "carrot and stick" approach that has helped to encourage corporate sourcing of renewables in other countries. For example, Australia developed a renewable energy target scheme with financial incentives (e.g. solar subsidies) alongside industry obligations for renewable energy consumption. This helped to bring spot prices down for renewable electricity generation (via certificates) and led to development of 3.5 GW of new renewable generation capacity in 2020, supported notably by corporate PPAs (Kay, 2020[14]). Such incentives could be combined in the Colombian content to encourage further development of bioenergy projects. For instance, tax incentives and/or other financial support (e.g. concessional finance or direct subsidies) could be used to encourage bioenergy development alongside industry obligations to increase its share of renewable energy consumption.

## Stronger waste management regulation will encourage greater energy recovery

Colombia stands out amongst its regional peers for having a broad regulatory framework on waste management as well as for having a waste management sector that is primarily operated by private entities. The regulatory statute under Presidential Decree 1076 of 2015[23] incorporates measures to prevent mismanagement of waste and hazardous refuse, aiming notably to protect the environment and human health. It complements the previous Decree 838 of 2005[24] and later Resolution 1890 of 2011[25] which prohibited uncontrolled burning, dumping and temporary trenching of waste. Decree 2820 of 2010[26] similarly prohibited release of waste into bodies of water, and additional regulations such as Decree 2981 of 2013[27] and Decree 596 of 2016[28] provide for overall public sanitation services.

The result is that around 83% of municipal solid waste (MSW) is collected and disposed of in official landfills (RVO, 2021[7]). Disposal regulations also allow for cost recovery through collection tariffs, providing sufficient financial sustainability for these services. Specifically, Law 142 of 1994 and regulations such as Resolution 720 of 2015[29] and Resolution 853 of 2018[30] provided a basis for the provision of municipal services through competing companies with tariffs that are cross-subsidised across the socio-economic strata (Calderón Márquez and Rutkowski, 2020[15]). This allows 99% of municipalities to have waste collection services.

At the same time, close to 50% of landfill sites in Colombia will reach capacity over the next decade, and constraints on new disposal sites, due to public opinion and evolving regulation, mean there is a growing need for sustainable waste management practices. In recent years, the government has sought to prioritise waste-to-energy, recycling and composting through its 2016 policy on integrated management of solid waste policy (Política Nacional Para La Gestión Integral de Residuos Sólidos[31]) and the 2019 Circular Economy Strategy. Both aim to increase the rate of recycling and waste utilisation across the country, from 8.7% in 2020 to 17.9% in 2030 (RVO, 2021[7]).

### *The cost of waste disposal directly influences appetite for bioenergy solutions*

The incentive for sorting and recovery of waste, despite a strong policy framework and policy ambitions, remains low. Landfill and waste collection fees are set by the Commission for the Regulation of Drinking Water and Basic Sanitation and apply to the amount of waste collected or disposed of. Waste management and landfill operators consequently have little incentive to reduce waste as this would impact their revenue streams, especially as most operations are privately owned.

In addition, landfill and waste collection fees are typically low. On average, waste disposal in landfills has a fee of around USD 9.5 per tonne, compared to higher rates such as those used at Bogotá's Doña Juana site, which has fees around USD 16 per tonne (RVO, 2021[7]). By comparison, average disposal costs in the European Union, where waste-to-energy applications are more common, are about USD 60 per tonne (CEWEP, 2020[16]). In European countries with high shares (i.e. >50%) of waste-to-energy treatment (e.g. Denmark, Finland and Sweden), gate fees and landfill taxes are more than USD 120 per tonne (IEA, 2020[17]).

To direct waste streams from landfills towards recycling and energy recovery, Colombia should continue to review waste fees and related market incentives. The Ministry of Housing, City and Territory already introduced a landfill tax in 2020, initially set at around USD 2 per tonne (RVO, 2021[7]). Progressively increasing the value of the tax will provide improved price signals that will encourage greater sorting and treatment of waste, as the current tax is only a marginal increase above current average disposal fees. This would also help to drive new business models around the sorting, recycling, and recovery of waste (e.g. in industry co-processing), where sorting and treatment are an essential step for waste-to-energy projects, as large quantities of organic and non-flammable materials in waste can lead to insufficiently high temperatures for energy production. They can also contribute to toxic emissions during incineration, which have led to public resistance and protests from public health concerns over waste-to-energy projects in countries such as Thailand (Weatherby, 2019[18]).

Given organic residues account for about 60% of MSW in Colombia (Government of Colombia, 2019[19]), sorting and treatment of MSW will play a critical role in enabling effective and efficient waste-to-energy solutions. This includes applications for energy-intensive industries such as cement production, which requires sorted and treated waste of known composition to be suitable for the combustion process and clinker sintering (Jovovic, 2017[20]). Treatment of other forms of refuse like hazardous industrial waste is equally important for these to be used as feedstock, although again, price signals under current regulations for hazardous waste do not sufficiently encourage treatment for recovery in energy production.

The regulatory framework for hazardous waste management in Colombia follows the international Basel Convention with rules and information on the quantities of hazardous waste generated (Ordoñez-Ordoñez, Echeverry-Lopera and Colorado-Lopera, 2019[21]). Notably, Decree 4741 of 2005[32] regulated the prevention and management of hazardous waste, and Ministry of Environment and Sustainable Development (Ministerio de Ambiente y Desarrollo Sostenible, MADS) Resolution 1362 of 2007[33] established the requirements and procedures for generators of hazardous waste to be listed in the Ministry's registry. A number of additional regulations,[34] for instance on equipment and refuse that contain or are contaminated with polychlorinated biphenyls, set requirements for the comprehensive environmental management of hazardous waste and Colombia stands out amongst regional peers for overall industry compliance.

Compliance with existing regulatory requirements may be high, but there nonetheless is little incentive to invest in waste-to-energy solutions, given the comparatively low costs of hazardous waste treatment and disposal, even when in specialised, secure landfills (RVO, 2021[7]). In fact, of the nearly 670 thousand tonnes of hazardous waste generated in 2019, nearly half went to final disposal in secure landfills (IDEAM, 2020[22]). Another 40% was treated (e.g. through pre-remediation and physical-chemical processes), and only 13% was actually recovered for other uses, for instance in energy production. Moreover, recovery of hazardous wastes with typically high calorific values (e.g. from the petroleum oil and chemical industries) was less than 2%, underscoring the lack of regulatory and financial impetus for energy recovery applications.

### *Firm disposal rules and higher fees will improve the business case for waste recovery*

MADS policy on extended producer responsibility has helped to improve motivation with some producers to recover and treat certain hazardous wastes such as electrical and electronic equipment and batteries, although participation is voluntary (RVO, 2021[7]). The National Business Association of Colombia (Asociación Nacional de Empresarios de Colombia) has equally led some programmes to encourage recovery of post-consumer materials, although this has not necessarily led to any significant changes in industrial waste management.

Strengthening these initiatives, for instance through firm targets or mandatory retrieval of certain wastes, can help to increase overall treatment and recovery, as has been the case in other countries. For example, some extended producer responsibility policies have end-of-life requirements (e.g. through eco-fees or mandatory deposit-refund schemes) to encourage waste retrieval, treatment and recovery.[35] Europe, the United States, Japan, Korea and Brazil, for instance, have end-of-life tyre regulations in place to ensure their proper management, treatment and re-use (e.g. in energy and material recovery) in lieu of landfilling (WBCSD, 2019[23]).[36] This has encouraged development of opportunities for waste-to-energy applications, where by example, 94% of all end-of-life tyres in Europe were collected and treated in 2019, with 40% used for energy recovery (ETRMA, 2021[24]).

Increasing the scope and stringency of the regulatory framework for waste management and recovery in Colombia will encourage similar development of potential waste-to-energy solutions This will equally help to build the business case for expansion of industry experiences with such investments. For example, the cement company, Argos, developed co-processing capacity at two of its cement plants in Rioclaro and Cartagena, using more than 75 thousand tonnes of waste as an alternative fuel in 2018 (Stewardson, 2019[25]). MADS regulations already legally recognised this co-processing as a sustainable alternative under Resolution 909 of 2008[37] (later modified by Resolution 802 of 2014[38]), but there are no requirements or incentives to seek out such use of refuse-derived fuels. More stringent policies for waste disposal, recycling and recovery (e.g. for tyre manufactures or hazardous industrial waste) would consequently encourage a clearer supply chain and better business model for further alternative fuel applications in cement manufacturing (see Annex A on refuse-derived fuel use for cement manufacturing in Brazil).

Improved price regimes for waste collection services and landfill tipping fees can also support development of recovery and waste-to-energy capacity. This can be through direct pricing, building upon the recently announced landfill tax, or through use of differentiated fee scales for certain types of waste (e.g. high gate fees for hazardous wastes to urge greater treatment and recovery). Additional regulatory signals, such as development of a mandatory emissions trading scheme or carbon pricing that encompasses fossil fuel use in industry, would also provide incentive for waste recovery and re-use, so long as measures are complimented by clear regulation on future landfill disposal (i.e. avoiding a “chicken and egg” situation in which demand for waste is not matched by needs for alternatives to disposal).

The value of these potential price signals is already evident in waste-to-energy applications such as the Bogotá Doña Juana landfill, which is registered as a project under the United Nations Clean Development Mechanism to manage fugitive methane emission. Between 2009 and 2016, the project had already earned 4.6 million emissions reduction certificates from its use of methane to produce power for electricity supply to around four thousand households (Cruz, 2021[26]). The credits, which generate around USD 780 thousand per year in revenue for the project and the city, illustrate the opportunity for similar applications (e.g. the landfill biogas project that will be developed in Medellín) to benefit from carbon trading and/or global climate funds through such emissions reduction credits (Contreras et al., 2020[27]).

Lastly, the government can work with related industry associations to identify opportunities and additional regulatory barriers to waste-to-energy development. For example, the Latin American Cement Association (La Federación Interamericana del Cemento) has actively explored co-processing through its working groups since 2010, and these discussions have helped to inform regulatory frameworks in support of redirecting waste streams towards energy recovery within industry.[39] These types of dialogues can strengthen the regulatory link between waste and industry in Colombia, thereby helping to support development of a policy environment and market signals that enable practical and effective waste-to-energy solutions.

## References

Alzate-Arias, S. et al. (2018), "Assessment of government incentives for energy from waste in Colombia", *Sustainability (Switzerland)*, Vol. 10/4, http://dx.doi.org/10.3390/SU10041294. [6]

Asocaña (2021), *Annual Report (Informe Annual) 2020-2021*, Colombian Sugarcane Growers Association (Asociación de Cultivadores de Caña de Azúcar, Asocaña), https://www.asocana.org/documentos/1782021-3772D9B2-00FF00,000A000,878787,C3C3C3,FF00FF,2D2D2D,A3C4B5.pdf (accessed on 8 September 2021). [2]

Asocaña (2014), *The Colombian sugar sector, more than sugar, a renewable energy source for the country: co-generation (Cogeneracion - El Sector Azucarero Colombiano, más que azúcar, una fuente de energía renovable para el país)*, Colombian Sugarcane Growers Association (Asociación de Cultivadores de Caña de Azúcar, Asocaña), https://www.asocana.org/documentos/2692014-90F926BD-00FF00,000A000,878787,C3C3C3,0F0F0F,B4B4B4,FF00FF,2D2D2D.pdf (accessed on 15 September 2021). [4]

Calderón Márquez, A. and E. Rutkowski (2020), "Waste management drivers towards a circular economy in the global south – The Colombian case", *Waste Management*, Vol. 110, pp. 53-65, http://dx.doi.org/10.1016/J.WASMAN.2020.05.016. [15]

CCC (2016), "Cámara de Comercio de Cali", *Cali Chamber of Commerce (Cámara de Comercio de Cali, CCC) Rhythm Cluster (Ritmo Cluster)* 03, https://www.ccc.org.co/inc/uploads/informes-economicos/ritmo-cluster/3.pdf?__cf_chl_captcha_tk__=pmd_InPQWtyNiusgTdfX_gAHa6ciIY8LFy.akEfLyB1rk7w-1632660979-0-gqNtZGzNAyWjcnBszQbI (accessed on 26 September 2021). [1]

CEIA (2019), *CEIA Colombia: Accelerating Solar Energy for Commercial and Industrial Customers*, Clean Energy Investment Accelerator (CEIA), https://static1.squarespace.com/static/5b7e51339772aebd21642486/t/5d8bc01583efb753866468b6/1569439766107/CEIA+Colombia_One+Pager+Sept+2019.pdf (accessed on 29 September 2021). [11]

CEWEP (2020), *Landfill Taxes and Bans*, The Confederation of European Waste-to-Energy Plants (CEWEP), https://www.cewep.eu/landfill-taxes-and-bans/ (accessed on 27 September 2021). [16]

Contreras, M. et al. (2020), "A look to the biogas generation from organic wastes in Colombia", *International Journal of Energy Economics and Policy*, Vol. 10/5, pp. 248-254, http://dx.doi.org/10.32479/IJEEP.9639. [27]

Cruz, M. (2021), *Did you know that in Doña Juana the gases from organic waste are used? (¿Sabías que en Doña Juana se aprovechan los gases de los residuos orgánicos?)*, Bogota.gov.co, https://bogota.gov.co/mi-ciudad/habitat/planta-de-biogas-dona-juana-en-bogota (accessed on 15 September 2021). [26]

Duarte, S., B. Loaiza and A. Majano (2021), *From practice to politics: analysis of investment barriers for biogas in Colombia and measures to address them, based on the experience of developers and other relevant actors (De la práctica a la política: análisis de las barreras a la inversión en biogás en Colombia y las medidas para abordarlas, a partir de la experiencia de los desarrolladores y otros actores relevantes)*, LEDS-LAC, https://ledslac.org/wp-content/uploads/2021/08/Informe-final-biogas-Colombia-v.06082021-final.pdf (accessed on 16 September 2021). [8]

ETRMA (2021), *In Europe 94% of all End of Life Tyres were collected and treated in 2019*, European Tyre and Rubber Manufacturers' Association, https://www.etrma.org/wp-content/uploads/2021/05/20210511_ETRMA_PRESS-RELEASE_ELT-2019.pdf (accessed on 15 September 2021). [24]

Government of Colombia (2019), *National Circular Economy Strategy Content: closing of material cycles, technological innovation, collaboration and new business models (Estrategia Nacional de Economía Circular Contenido: cierre de ciclos de materiales, innovación tecnológica, colaboración y nuevos modelos de negocio)*, Ministry of Environment and Sustainable Development (Ministerio de Ambiente y Desarrollo Sustenible) and Ministry of Commerce, Trade and Tourism (Ministerio de Comercio, Industria y Turismo), http://www.andi.com.co/Uploads/Estrategia%20Nacional%20de%20EconA%CC%83%C2%B3mia%20Circular-2019%20Final.pdf_637176135049017259.pdf (accessed on 16 September 2021). [19]

IDEAM (2020), *National report on hazardous waste and residuals in Colombia, 2019 (Informe nacional de residuos o desechos peligrosos en Colombia, 2019)*, Institute of Hydrology, Meteorology and Environmental Studies (Instituto de Hidrología, Meteorología y Estudios Ambientales, IDEAM), http://documentacion.ideam.gov.co/openbiblio/bvirtual/023901/InformeResiduos2019.pdf (accessed on 27 September 2021). [22]

IEA (2020), *Sustainable Bioenergy for Georgia: A Roadmap*, International Energy Agency (IEA), Paris, https://www.iea.org/reports/sustainable-bioenergy-for-georgia-a-roadmap (accessed on 27 September 2021). [17]

IETA (2021), *Carbon Market Business Brief: Colombia*, International Emissions Trading Association (IETA), https://ieta.org/resources/Resources/CarbonMarketBusinessBrief/2021/CarbonMarketBusinessBrief_Colombia2021.pdf (accessed on 22 September 2021). [12]

Jovovic, A. (2017), *Possibilities and effects of using waste materials as energy in cement industry*, Balkan Green Energy News, https://balkangreenenergynews.com/possibilities-effects-using-waste-materials-energy-cement-industry/ (accessed on 27 September 2021). [20]

Kay, I. (2020), *Attracting Private Investment for Renewable Energy*, Australian Renewable Energy Agency (ARENA), https://www.slideshare.net/OECD_ENV/ppt-ian-kay-attracting-private-investment-for-renewable-energy (accessed on 16 December 2020). [14]

Morganstein, J. et al. (2021), "Renewable Energy Procurement Guidebook for Colombia", *World Resources Institute*, http://dx.doi.org/10.46830/WRIGB.19.00129. [10]

Ordoñez-Ordoñez, E., G. Echeverry-Lopera and H. Colorado-Lopera (2019), "Engineering and economics of the hazardous wastes in Colombia: the need for a circular economy model", *Informador Técnico*, Vol. 83/2, pp. 155-173, http://dx.doi.org/10.23850/22565035.2041. [21]

Riley and P. Zarnowiecki (2012), "Overview of UK Offshore Wind Market", *Orrick*, https://www.orrick.com/api/content/downloadattachment?id=bb4e5e43-95f6-4b55-ac4f-59d4838f64e8. [13]

RVO (2021), *Waste Management in the LATAM Region: Business Opportunities for the Netherlands in waste/circular economy sector in eight countries of Latin America*, The Netherlands Enterprise Agency (RVO), https://www.rvo.nl/sites/default/files/2021/02/Report_LATAM_Waste_Management_feb_2021.pdf (accessed on 16 September 2021). [7]

Sanchez Molina, P. (2020), *Colombia streamlines tax incentives for renewables*, PV Magazine, https://www.pv-magazine.com/2020/06/16/colombia-streamlines-tax-incentives-for-renewables/ (accessed on 17 September 2021). [5]

Stewardson, L. (2019), *Cementos Argos increases waste co-processing capacity in Colombia*, World Cement, https://www.worldcement.com/the-americas/10052019/cementos-argos-increases-waste-co-processing-capacity-in-colombia/ (accessed on 27 September 2021). [25]

UPME (2021), *Self-generation and distributed generation requests 2021 (Solicitudes de autogeneración y generación distribuida 2021)*, Planning Unit of the Ministry of Mines and Energy (Unidad de Planeación Minero Energética, UPME), https://public.tableau.com/app/profile/upme/viz/AutogeneracionyGeneracionDistribuida2021/Historia1 (accessed on 17 September 2021). [9]

WBCSD (2019), "Global ELT Management - A global state of knowledge on regulation, management systems, impacts of recovery and technologies", *World Business Council for Sustainable Development (WBCSD)*, p. 57, https://docs.wbcsd.org/2019/12/Global_ELT_Management%E2%80%93A_global_state_of_knowledge_on_regulation_management_systems_impacts_of_recovery_and_technologies.pdf (accessed on 27 September 2021). [23]

Weatherby, C. (2019), *Waste-to-energy: A renewable opportunity for Southeast Asia?*, Eco-Business, https://www.eco-business.com/news/waste-to-energy-a-renewable-opportunity-for-southeast-asia/ (accessed on 27 September 2021). [18]

XM (2021), *Generación SIN*, Indicatores, https://www.xm.com.co/Paginas/Indicadores/Oferta/Indicador-generacion-sin.aspx (accessed on 5 October 2021). [3]

## Notes

[1] For more information (in Spanish), see: https://www.funcionpublica.gov.co/eva/gestornormativo/norma.php?i=4449.

[2] For more information (in Spanish), see: http://apolo.creg.gov.co/Publicac.nsf/1c09d18d2d5ffb5b05256eee00709c02/0a6fcadc48be17910525785a007a5ce5?OpenDocument and http://apolo.creg.gov.co/Publicac.nsf/Indice01/Resoluci%C3%B3n-1996-CRG86-96.

[3] For more information (in Spanish), see: http://apolo.creg.gov.co/PUBLICAC.NSF/Indice01/Resoluci%C3%B3n-1998-CREG107-98.

[4] For more information (in Spanish), see: https://www.funcionpublica.gov.co/eva/gestornormativo/norma.php?i=7260.

[5] For more information (in Spanish), see: https://www.funcionpublica.gov.co/eva/gestornormativo/norma.php?i=31427.

[6] For more information (in Spanish), see: http://apolo.creg.gov.co/Publicac.nsf/Indice01/Resolucion-2010-Creg005-2010.

[7] The 2010-15 PROURE programme was later extended to 2022 under MME Resolution 41286 of 2016. For more information (in Spanish), see: https://www1.upme.gov.co/DemandaEnergetica/MarcoNormatividad/plan.pdf and https://www1.upme.gov.co/Paginas/PROURE.aspx.

[8] For further information (in Spanish), see: http://www.suin-juriscol.gov.co/clp/contenidos.dll/Resolucion/4020552?fn=document-frame.htm$f=templates$3.0.

[9] Reactive power is the power that flows back towards the grid in an alternating current scenario.

[10] For more information (in Spanish), see: http://apolo.creg.gov.co/Publicac.nsf/1c09d18d2d5ffb5b05256eee00709c02/65f1aaf1d57726a90525822900064dac/$FILE/Creg015-2018.pdf and http://apolo.creg.gov.co/Publicac.nsf/1c09d18d2d5ffb5b05256eee00709c02/83b41035c2c4474f05258243005a1191/$FILE/Creg030-2018.pdf.

[11] For more information (in Spanish), see: https://www.funcionpublica.gov.co/eva/gestornormativo/norma.php?i=85659.

[12] For more information (in Spanish), see: https://www.funcionpublica.gov.co/eva/gestornormativo/norma.php?i=166326.

[13] For more information (in Spanish), see: http://apolo.creg.gov.co/Publicac.nsf/1c09d18d2d5ffb5b05256eee00709c02/dafe4d4fc83940e2052580bf005b67d0?OpenDocument.

[14] For more information (in Spanish), see: https://www.funcionpublica.gov.co/eva/gestornormativo/norma.php?i=64682.

[15] For more information (in Spanish), see: https://dapre.presidencia.gov.co/normativa/normativa/DECRETO%20829%20DEL%2010%20DE%20JUNIO%20DE%202020.pdf.

[16] For more information (in Spanish), see: https://www.funcionpublica.gov.co/eva/gestornormativo/norma.php?i=137050.

[17] For more information (in Spanish), see: http://extwprlegs1.fao.org/docs/pdf/col146970.pdf.

[18] For more information (in Spanish), see: https://www.incp.org.co/Site/2016/info/archivos/resolucion-045-minminas.pdf.

[19] For more information (in Spanish), see: http://apolo.creg.gov.co/Publicac.nsf/1c09d18d2d5ffb5b05256eee00709c02/65f1aaf1d57726a90525822900064dac/$FILE/Creg015-2018.pdf and https://gestornormativo.creg.gov.co/gestor/entorno/docs/resolucion_creg_0030_2016.htm.

[20] For more information (in Spanish), see: https://www.minenergia.gov.co/documents/10180/23517/48221-Res+MME+40715+10+Sep+2019.pdf.

[21] Regulated electricity customers have a peak demand less than 100 kilowatts and monthly energy consumption less than 55 thousand kWh. Commercial and industrial users with demand over 100 kilowatts and/or monthly energy consumption over 55 thousand kWh can also choose this structure (they are automatically enrolled as long as they are connected to the grid) or they can chose to be unregulated consumers, allowing them to negotiate with a retailer or to establish direct agreements with a generator.

[22] For more information (in Spanish), see: http://es.presidencia.gov.co/normativa/normativa/DECRETO%20926%20DEL%2001%20DE%20JUNIO%20DE%202017.pdf.

[23] For more information (in Spanish), see: https://www.funcionpublica.gov.co/eva/gestornormativo/norma.php?i=78153.

[24] For more information (in Spanish), see: https://www.minambiente.gov.co/images/BosquesBiodiversidadyServiciosEcosistemicos/pdf/Normativa/Decretos/dec_0838_230305.pdf.

[25] For more information (in Spanish), see: https://eeppdelaceja.gov.co/download/resolucion-1890-de-2011-alternativas-para-la-disposicion-final-de-residuos/.

[26] For more information (in Spanish), see: https://www.funcionpublica.gov.co/eva/gestornormativo/norma.php?i=45524.

[27] For more information (in Spanish), see: https://www.suin-juriscol.gov.co/viewDocument.asp?id=1505864.

[28] For more information (in Spanish), see: https://www.funcionpublica.gov.co/eva/gestornormativo/norma.php?i=69038.

[29] For more information (in Spanish), see: https://www.cra.gov.co/documents/RESOLUCION-720-DE-2015-EDICION-Y-COPIA.pdf.

[30] For more information (in Spanish), see: https://www.cra.gov.co/documents/RESOLUCION_CRA_853_DE_2018.pdf.

[31] For more information (in Spanish), see: https://colaboracion.dnp.gov.co/CDT/Conpes/Econ%C3%B3micos/3874.pdf.

[32] For more information (in Spanish), see: http://www.suin-juriscol.gov.co/viewDocument.asp?ruta=Decretos/1879924.

[33] For more information (in Spanish), see: http://www.ideam.gov.co/documents/51310/526371/Resolucion+1362+2007++REQUISITOS+Y+PROCEDIMIENTOS+PARA+REG+DE+GENERADORES+DE+RESPEL.pdf/cdd6d851-013b-4bea-adf6-addec449f32b.

[34] For more information (in Spanish), see: https://www.car.gov.co/vercontenido/2542 and http://documentacion.ideam.gov.co/openbiblio/bvirtual/023901/InformeResiduos2019.pdf.

[35] For more information on extended producer responsibility policies, see: https://www.oecd.org/env/tools-evaluation/extendedproducerresponsibility.htm.

[36] For more information on global end-of-life tyre management practices, see the World Business Council for Sustainable Development (WBCSD) Tire Industry Project: https://www.wbcsd.org/Sector-Projects/Tire-Industry-Project/End-of-Life-Tires-ELTs.

[37] For more information (in Spanish), see: https://www.minambiente.gov.co/images/normativa/app/resoluciones/f0-Resoluci%C3%B3n%20909%20de%202008%20%20-%20Normas%20y%20estandares%20de%20emisi%C3%B3n%20Fuentes%20fijas.pdf.

[38] For more information (in Spanish), see: https://www.minambiente.gov.co/images/normativa/app/resoluciones/9b-Resoluci%C3%B3n%20802%20de%202014%20-%20Modifica%20parcialmente%20Resoluci%C3%B3n%20909%20de%202008.pdf.

[39] For more information (in Spanish), see: https://ficem.org/coprocesamiento-de-residuos-en-america-latina/.

# 4 Improved competition, innovation and finance for bioenergy development

Colombia has implemented a number of measures to increase the attractiveness of the country's investment environment, which has enabled increasing levels of private capital to be mobilised for renewable energy developments in recent years. Yet, investment in bioenergy projects, which struggle to compete with fossil fuels and the diminishing costs of solar and wind, remains limited. This is compounded by limited local technical expertise to implement projects and perceptions of risks by financial actors regarding bioenergy technologies and the stability of revenue streams from these additions. Addressing these issues requires efforts to increase awareness and familiarity with bioenergy solutions whilst improving overall access to finance, for instance by extending public support and development funds to de-risking tools for bioenergy projects. Use of capital market instruments like green bond issuance can also help to unlock affordable finance for bioenergy projects and to increase the investor base for clean energy solutions in Colombia.

## Highlights

- Competition with fossil fuels, low landfill fees and diminishing solar and wind costs have made it challenging to attract finance and investment for bioenergy projects. Supporting these capacity additions requires targeted measures to facilitate their access to market, including possible design elements in renewable energy auctions that attract smaller players or that reward projects based on criteria such as location and system friendliness.
- Bioenergy solutions can boost productivity and competitiveness, as has been the case with sugarcane and palm oil cogeneration additions. Awareness raising, capacity building and support for innovation will help enable local technical expertise and unlock opportunities for suitable bioenergy technologies, such as biodigesters for small-scale applications.
- The cost of finance for bioenergy technologies can often be high, due in part to limited local experience, unfamiliarity with these projects and overall perceptions of risk by financial actors. Finance for projects can also be a challenge given the creditworthiness or lack of credit history of smaller borrowers, in addition to difficulties in demonstrating a clear revenue stream. Work with financial partners like Bancolombia, Bancoldex and Finagro can build upon existing concessional credit lines to raise awareness and capacity for bioenergy project development.
- Colombia has several funds designed to support clean energy projects, mostly in the form of grants, which limits the number of projects that can be supported. Applying these funds more strategically, for instance through de-risking tools such as guarantees and credit enhancement, can encourage more active participation of private capital for bioenergy solutions. The government can also work with multilateral and international funds to design blended finance mechanisms that can catalyse private finance for bioenergy development in Colombia.
- The capital market is not a significant source of funding for clean energy projects in Colombia but represents an untapped opportunity to increase long-term, affordable financing. Support for the early design and use of capital market instruments like green bond issuance can help unlock access to these markets and deepen the investor base for clean energy development.

Colombia has taken a number of measures to increase the attractiveness of its investment environment since the 1990s, and the country ranked 57th (out of 141 countries) in the World Economic Forum's 2019 Global Competitiveness Report (Schwab, 2019[1]), up from 68th in 2010 (Schwab, 2010[2]). Colombia's stable macroeconomic situation, its large internal market and its growing, dynamic business environment (each respectively ranked 43rd, 37th and 49th) have all helped to encourage investment in a number of critical sectors, including in clean energy development. Trade agreements, including 13 bilateral deals such as those with Canada (2011), the United States (2012), the European Union (2014) and South Korea (2016), have also increased the country's economic attractiveness.

Private investment in non-conventional renewable energy (NCRE) has continued to increase in recent years, driven in particular by attractive tax exemptions, updated regulations on bilateral contracts and the 2019 renewable energy auctions. Still, Colombia will need to attract greater amounts of capital, including from foreign sources, to realise its clean energy ambitions over the next decade and beyond. There remains ample opportunity to increase investment in clean energy projects and President Ivan Duque Marquez announced in March of 2021 that government would accelerate reforms to attract foreign direct investment (FDI) in clean energy generation (Espejo, 2021[3]). This is a positive affirmation of the country's determination to unlock its renewable energy potential, though achievement will hang on engagement of the private sector, including commercial and industrial users that account for more than half of Colombia's electricity demand (Morganstein et al., 2021[4]). Many of these large companies have already started to invest in clean energy solutions, as evidenced by bioenergy cogeneration in the sugar and palm industries and more recent corporate rooftop solar procurement.

This engagement of private capital, all the same, can improve considerably and investment in bioenergy, which currently is limited mostly to industry financing of cogeneration projects, does not reflect technical opportunities and political ambitions highlighted by the government. Competition with fossil fuels and low landfill fees, even in light of measures like the landmark 2014 Renewable Energy Law, have made it challenging to attract finance and investment for bioenergy projects. This is compounded by recent competition with diminishing solar and wind costs under the Planning Unit of the Ministry of Mines and Energy (Unidad de Planeación Minero Energética,UPME) renewable energy auctions, whose price per kilowatt produced does not readily reflect the broader socioeconomic value of bioenergy capacity, nor the opportunities for those additions to be used for other energy vectors (e.g. biogas and biofuels). Limited experience with some bioenergy solutions, such as agricultural biogas projects, also means that effort is needed to support capacity building, technical skills, technology development and/or adaptation to unlock these untapped opportunities.

Improving this situation will require a more competitive market framework with improved access to affordable finance and greater support for innovation. For example, improved transparency in the UPME project registry and connection approval process will help to encourage greater participation of bioenergy projects. Targeted procurement of bioenergy development, for instance for local electricity generation capacity improvements, including in non-interconnected zones (zonas no interconectadas, ZNI), under the provisions under Law 2036 of 2020 to support territorial development of NCRE, can equally help to create a clear pipeline of new projects. Awareness building and technical training (e.g. for installation and operation of bioenergy technologies with local industry and farmers) will also increase capacity for project development. These types of actions will help to build upon existing regulatory measures and incentives to level the playing field for new bioenergy projects, whilst improving the interest and ability to deliver "bankable" project proposals and viable business models that are "investor ready".

## Fair market competition will improve the business case for bioenergy projects

Colombia's unbundled electricity market allows for private investment across the sector's activities and multiple actors contribute to generation, transmission, distribution and retail services. Electricity market reforms since the mid-1990s helped to introduce competition in the sector and foreign investors can also participate in the market, receiving the same treatment as Colombian nationals. In particular, FDI in electricity generation has very low restrictiveness, even if some issues remain, for instance the efficiency of the legal framework for dispute resolution (OECD, 2021[5]).

At the same time, the national electricity market has nonetheless struggled to provide a reliable supply of electricity under competitive conditions (World Bank, 2019[6]). Events like the 2016 El Niño crisis also have meant that consumers have faced significant price volatility where for example commercial and industrial electricity rates varied as much as 55% and 35% over 2010 tariffs (Morganstein et al., 2021[4]). In addition to structural weakness like the 2016 reliability market failures, market power also remains quite concentrated. Notably, more than 60% of generation capacity is owned by four actors (i.e. Emgesa, ISAGEN, Energía del Pacífico and the publicly owned company, EPM) who also participate in other electricity market activities.

Three additional companies control a further 16% of generation capacity and also have stakes in transmission, distribution and retail activities. The 2020 failure and liquidation of Electrocaribe (a large distribution company) meant that 68% of distribution is likewise owned by three firms (EPM, Condesa and Celsia). This concentration, alongside continued price volatility, illustrates that the unbundling of electricity market activities did not necessarily address the strong vertical and horizontal integration of the market, which in turn influences overall competitiveness and can discourage new actors. Market concentration problems (e.g. abuse of market power during tight demand-supply conditions) have also led to distorted tariffs and spot and contract prices (World Bank, 2019[6]).

### *The wholesale market is open, but options are limited for some bioenergy projects*

2018 reforms by the Superintendence of Industry and Trade (Superintendencia de Industria y Comercio)[1] helped to improve the overall, competitive framework for investments, for example by increasing investigations into bid-rigging with consequent sanctions. Ministry of Mines and Energy (Ministerio de Minas y Energía, MME) Decree 570 of 2018 and its power purchase agreement (PPA) guidance also helped to enable new electricity market entries, where notably, long-term contract mechanisms were previously a significant barrier to renewable energy additions. Specifically, bilateral contracts between generators and retailers often took the form of a take-or-pay contract, typically with a short duration of one or two years (World Bank, 2019[6]).

MME Decree 570 of 2018 addressed this by allowing generators to participate in the wholesale market via short-term and long-term transactions through firm energy obligations (under reliability auctions), in bilateral contracts or via the spot market. Bilateral contracts in particular have worked well for utility-scale additions such as those signed under the 2019 and 2021 renewable energy auctions, which helped to draw in foreign investors, who represented over half of the participant awards. The utility-scale bilateral agreements also helped retailers to fulfil their renewable portfolio requirements (see regulatory section above) by securing sizeable PPAs with typically large and experienced players. In fact, awarded contracts in the 2019 auctions were only capacities above 75 MW, even if the capacity floor for bids was set at 5 MW.

Technically, bilateral contracts with smaller players and generation sizes are possible, but these can be challenging, especially for less established actors. This is particularly the case for opportunities to engage with unregulated customers, who can only contract via a single retailer under Energy and Gas Regulation Commission (Comisión de Regulación de Energía y Gas, CREG) Resolution 131 of 1998.[2] This effectively requires smaller generators to find a retailer willing to act as the conduit to supply electricity to unregulated customers. Additionally, the retailer also needs to agree to provide the customer's remaining electricity needs, should the generator not have sufficiently installed capacity (Morganstein et al., 2021[4]). It is therefore easier for larger generators to negotiate these types of bilateral contracts, especially if they have integrated retail activities, allowing them to contract directly with unregulated customers.

Beyond bilateral agreements, another option is for generators to sell their electricity directly in the spot market. This can include self-generators, as long as they are connected to the grid and are above 2 MW, as well as distributed generation projects that are over 20 MW. This option can work well for generators with existing surplus capacity (e.g. in industry cogeneration) and can even compliment bilateral contract agreements (see Annex A on sugarcane cogeneration in Colombia). Yet, the spot market by itself does not provide sufficient visibility in medium- to long-term pricing (nor eventual demand) to justify capital expenditures for new capacity additions, as price predictability not only is critical to justify upfront capital needs but also helps to hedge against potential operational fluctuations (e.g. in feedstock prices for biogas generation). Given retailer preferences for bilateral contracts with larger utility-scale additions, this gap between the spot market and PPAs effectively leaves smaller-scale projects in a challenging space to secure a clear revenue stream.

Firm energy obligations, by comparison, can provide more attractive terms for such projects, as the obligations include a stable reliability payment in USD over a 20-year period. Yet, the firm energy auctions by themselves may not provide sufficient revenue to attract new capacity additions. Additionally, incumbent actors' concentration in the generation market gives those companies a natural advantage and firm energy auctions have consequently lacked competition (World Bank, 2019[6]). This was evident in the price spikes of 2016, where greater inclusion of renewable energy in the reliability charges would have improved generator diversity and taken pressure off fossil fuels (particularly natural gas) in tight supply conditions.

Overall, the 2018 reforms may have opened the electricity market to new actors and foreign investment, but entry for smaller actors and generation projects is still challenging. This applies to bioenergy projects, which in addition to competing with solar and wind prices in the renewable energy auctions also lack a clear pathway to sales in the wider wholesale market. Efforts to create a more level playing field for all types and size of generators will therefore be critical to improving the business case for investment in bioenergy projects.

### *Use of more targeted measures can facilitate bioenergy access to market*

One possible way to address this is to revisit design elements used in renewable energy auctions in order to support greater participation of bioenergy bids in future rounds. For example, buyers and sellers under the 2019 auctions had to submit commitment bonds as financial guarantees, where specifically sellers had to present a performance bond (garantía de cumplimiento) and a start-up guarantee (garantía de puesta en operación). These types of guarantees are commonly used to ensure an auction's success and to discourage underperformance of projects (IRENA and USAID, 2021[7]).Yet, stakeholders indicated after the first auction in February 2019 that the bond amounts for bidders were too high and could be difficult to obtain, especially on short notice. The amounts were subsequently lowered in the October 2019 and 2021 auctions, but they may still be a barrier for some bioenergy projects (amongst others), particularly where bioenergy technologies or applications have limited demonstration in the Colombian context and as a result may have difficulties obtaining necessary guarantees.

To address this, the government could consider acting as the guarantor of certain types of bioenergy projects (e.g. biogas capacity additions from agricultural or municipal waste streams). Future renewable energy auctions could also target design elements to attract smaller players, for instance by establishing winner selection criteria that compensate new and/or small developers beyond their pricing offers (IRENA and USAID, 2021[7]). Auction design could also include pricing that incorporates elements like a locational component, which is a feature in renewable energy auctions in Mexico, thereby increasing or decreasing the value of a bid depending on system friendliness. This has meant that even if some bid prices were more expensive, projects could still be selected over other less expensive ones if they had more value for the system (e.g. because the project was located in a place of power scarcity) (OECD, 2021[8]).

Future auctions could likewise apply criteria to reward projects based on their target bioenergy projects specifically (Box 4.1). For example, the government of Brazil announced in December 2020 that it would hold an auction specific to waste-to-energy projects in 2021 (ABREN, 2020[9]). Indonesia similarly held auctions for three waste-to-energy projects in 2019 and 2020, with further plants to develop 12 such generation plants (Lim, Yuen and Bhaskar, 2021[10]). These projects will help tap into large potential for bioenergy production and address challenges with price competition with other renewable energy sources.

Other procurement approaches such as public-private partnership (PPP) models can also help bioenergy developers to enter the market in light of current challenges to secure bilateral agreements with retailers (RVO, 2021[11]). For example, support for design-build-own-operate agreements through publicly owned utilities (e.g. EPM) could help bioenergy developers to access the market and demonstrate the value of these additions, whilst also supporting the projects to overcome other critical barriers, such as obtaining affordable financing without a clear pathway to a longer-term contractual agreement. These types of contractual structures can likewise be encouraged with private retailers, either through targeted support (e.g. fiscal incentives for retailers) or even specific portfolio requirements within current portfolio rules.

**Box 4.1. Promoting bioenergy development through targeted auctions in Brazil**

Bioenergy solutions can play an important role in meeting Brazil's growing electricity needs, given substantial agricultural and municipal waste streams in the country. For example, the country's local waste-to-energy association, Abren, identified as much as 5 GW of waste-to-energy capacity potential, which could meet up to 8% of national electricity demand. Unlocking this potential would require investment of around USD 30 billion (160 billion Brazilian real). Yet, as in many other countries, these potential bioenergy solutions have struggled to attract investment, given competition with other electricity generation sources and more recent renewable energy auctions, whose price schemes have not directly reflected the value added from improved waste management.

To enable development of these opportunities, Brazil's National Electricity Regulatory Agency (Agência Nacional de Energia Elétrica), tailored the design of its power generation auction in 2021 to help procure bioenergy capacity additions. This new bidding process was open to wind, solar, hydro and bioenergy projects (thermal plants using sugarcane bagasse, wood chips and solid urban waste) as well as coal and natural gas capacity. Yet, different price caps were applied by technology or groups of technologies, allowing for competition within these categories. Winning generators signed contracts directly with distribution companies, and PPAs will come into effect in January 2026.

The new auctions provided a specific price cap for waste-to-energy technologies, allowing these to compete against each other. The cap for solid waste projects was set to USD 118 per MWh, compared to the price set for wind and solar at USD 35 per MWh. Other bioenergy technologies such as sugar cane bagasse and wood chips fell within the thermal category, with a price cap of USD 67 per MWh. Additionally, while contracts for wind and solar secured 15-year terms, bioenergy and waste-to-energy plants were awarded 20-year contracts.

The newly designed auctions were held on 30 September 2021 and 861 MW of renewable energy projects were awarded at an average price of USD 44 per MWh. Within these newly secured PPAs, bioenergy projects were awarded the largest additions, securing 321 MW of future capacity.

In the face of recent hydro shortages, the government of Brazil also took the decision to hold a thermal auction for Brazil's capacity reserves. 132 energy projects (both new and existing) will compete for 51 GW of awarded contracts in the auction planned for December 2021. Natural gas accounts for the majority of bids, though a notable share of bioenergy projects are also in the running (amongst other technologies). In total, 437 MW of bioenergy capacity is registered to participate, including biofuels (269 MW), sugarcane bagasse (80 MW), municipal solid waste (45 MW), wood chips (25 MW) and biogas (18 MW).

This impressive shift in bioenergy projects participating in Brazil's energy auctions illustrates that tailoring procurement design (e.g. through technology specific price caps) can encourage participation of underrepresented technologies and increase contract awards to those projects. This targeted approach also helped to improve price discovery through narrower competition across project types.

Sources: (ABREN, 2021[12]); (REGlobal, 2021[13]); (Renewables Now, 2021[14]); (Renewables Now, 2021[15]); (BNAmericas, 2021[16])

## Innovation and capacity building can improve the business case for bioenergy

Colombia has an overall attractive investment environment, although there remain some challenges in attracting greater levels of private capital, including for clean energy development due to issues regarding productivity, given high levels of informality in parts of the country's economic structure (OECD, 2019[17]).

This includes low productivity undermining the agricultural sector's competitiveness and innovation capacity, which indirectly affects the attractiveness of investment in bioenergy solutions.

Short-term responses to problems faced by the sector have tended to focus on input subsidies, although a recent 2019 policy on contract farming did promote a longer-term linkage between small-scale producers and markets, for example promoting alliances between the agricultural and industrial sectors (OECD, 2020[18]). Additional measures targeting strategic investment in the sustainable development of the agricultural sector (e.g. strengthened policy regarding spending on innovation and advanced bioenergy technologies) would benefit related bioenergy capacity, such as anaerobic digestion technologies.

There equally is extensive opportunity to develop clean energy solutions that would boost overall industry sustainability and competitiveness in Colombia, for instance through bioenergy applications like the cogeneration capacities developed in the sugar and palm industries. Investment in these types of solutions remains limited across the various industrial sectors, reflecting wider market issues with respect to productivity and innovation in industry and agriculture (OECD, 2014[19]). Lack of familiarity and expertise amongst industry actors, for example for implementation and use of bioenergy technologies, also contributes to this weak deployment and requires further technical competence (RVO, 2021[11]).

These issues of low innovation and technical capacity were highlighted in the 2018 Green Growth Strategy, which subsequently prioritised actions to support science, technology and innovation, as well as the development of human capital to support green growth. Notably, the report highlighted that investment in science, technology and innovation is low (around 0.7% of GDP in 2016), and spending on innovation by the private sector is very low, with 54% of these investments between 2006 and 2016 coming from the public sector (DNP, 2018[20]). By contrast, around 70% of spending on research and innovation in OECD countries is made by the private sector (OECD, 2020[21]).

Increased investment in innovation can improve the business case for bioenergy projects in Colombia, including through development of cost-effective solutions that are adapted to the specific needs or context of the local application. For example, imported technology solutions may not be adapted to specific industry conditions or operating contexts (e.g. for use in small poultry and dairy farms). Development of suitable technologies (e.g. biodigesters for micro- and small-scale applications) will enable greater opportunities for bioenergy use in those industries. Investment support can equally target capacity building for local bioenergy production, for instance through domestic pellet production using lignocellulosic waste from industry and agriculture, which could be used as a substitute for fossil fuel thermal power generation. Innovation can also target solutions such as new business models to sort and treat various forms of waste.

Support is also needed to develop technical expertise, as local industry and agricultural actors can be unfamiliar with the installation, operations, maintenance, repairs and replacement of bioenergy technology. Awareness raising, alongside training and capacity building, can help to address these issues, whilst equally helping to identify and develop cost-effective solutions for local bioenergy projects, as those actors are more familiar with the operational application and technical needs. Support for local technical capacity will also help to increase economic productivity, as illustrated by the projects supported by the "Biovalor" initiative in Uruguay (see clean energy solutions above).

Innovation and capacity building efforts to enable bioenergy solutions in Colombia can build upon previous initiatives such as the 2014-18 national agenda for competition and innovation (Agenda Nacional de Competitividad e Innovación[3]). For example, the recently established Center for Industrial development (Centro de Desarrollo industrial, CENDI) can support innovation for bioenergy technologies by bringing together stakeholders and piloting bioenergy solutions for industry in Colombia. Engaging authorities such as the National Commission for Competition and Innovation (Comisión Nacional de Competitividad e Innovación[4]) and the national business and entrepreneurial promotion agency, iNNpulsa, can also help to encourage innovation for bioenergy solutions. These actors and initiatives can likewise support training, coaching services and other capacity building exercises to enable deployment of bioenergy technologies and business solutions in industry and other relevant sectors (e.g. agriculture).

The government can also consider the role of PPP models to enable bioenergy technology research, development, demonstration and deployment, for example through programmes supported by the Ministry of Science, Technology and Innovation (Ministerio de Ciencia Tecnología e Innovación). These can help to encourage private sector investment in bioenergy solutions in early market stages or where there is limited market experience, whilst enabling greater national expertise in solutions that can more efficiently (re)utilise Colombia's abundant waste resources for energy production.

Limited public resources can also be used to support critical stages of clean energy solutions and business ventures, for instance through targeted coaching and business development support. These targeted measures can help to ensure successful innovation, start-ups and scale-up of clean energy solutions, as has been the case in other countries (Box 4.2). They can also spur greater development of domestic supply chains and clean energy entrepreneurs, for instance helping firms to overcome the "valley of death".

### Box 4.2. InnoEnergy services through the European Institute of Innovation and Technology

The European Institute of Innovation and Technology (EIT) is an initiative that brings together actors to create Knowledge and Innovation Communities in support of technology research, development, demonstration and deployment across the European Union. The initiative was established by the European Parliament under Regulation No. 294 of 2008 with the ambition to connect businesses, entrepreneurs, researchers and other market actors through EIT's knowledge-sharing communities. Notably, these groups aim to support commercialisation and deployment of innovative technologies and encourage solutions by improving access to research findings, resources, networks and market opportunities.

EIT InnoEnergy[5] is one such community that prioritises clean energy solutions. This includes three specific industrial alliances targeting battery storage, green hydrogen and solar PV, where InnoEnergy aims to support innovations in these fields with the objective to provide industry with new technologies that decrease emissions and advance sustainability, whilst reducing energy costs, increasing system performance and improving industry competitiveness.

To achieve its ambition to catalyse and accelerate the clean energy transition, InnoEnergy provides support through a number of mechanisms, including finance through its InnoEnergy funds, loans and even venture capital. Bespoke support also includes assistance as needed for technical and business development and EIT provides equally opportunities for networking through events organised with industrial actors and investors.

By providing facilitated support and linkages between researchers, innovators and businesses, EIT has encouraged innovation in a number of clean energy sectors, including renewable energies, energy storage, sustainable cities and buildings, sustainable energy for transport and mobility, smart grids, and energy efficiency. To date, InnoEnergy has provided around EUR 560 million to more than 480 innovative solutions, helping clean energy developers to raise more than EUR 2.5 billion in total financing. These solutions are expected to generate about EUR 16 billion in commercial revenues by 2026 and, by 2030, companies supported by EIT are slated to save more than one billion tonnes of $CO_2$-equivalent, whilst saving industry around EUR 9 billion in energy costs.

Source: (InnoEnergy, 2020[22]) (InnoEnergy, 2021[23])

## Improved access to finance will increase capacity for bioenergy development

Colombia has taken a number of measures in recent years to address the role of finance in achieving its sustainable development goals and clean energy ambitions. This includes measures implemented by the Colombian Banking Association, Asobancaria, to promote better management, monitoring and reporting of environmental and social risks (IFC, 2018[24]). For instance, Asobancaria developed a voluntary Green Protocol (Protocolo Verde[6]) in 2012, which 13 banking institutions have since adopted (UNEP, 2021[25]). Asobancaria also issued detailed guidance on applying the Protocol in its 2016 General Guidelines for the Implementation of Environmental and Social Risk (Guía General de Implementación y Administración de Riesgos Ambientales y Sociales[7]).

Other initiatives, such as the government's National System for Climate Change (Sistema Nacional de Cambio Climático, SISCLIMA),[8] have improved ministerial co-ordination and public-private dialogue on climate finance to support project pipeline development. In 2018, SISCLIMA released a roadmap[9] for the development of green financial products (green bonds). This roadmap put forward actions to set the market foundations and to promote strategies for a strong green bonds market, building upon early issuances by the banks Bancolombia (2016), Davivienda and Bancóldex (2017) (IFC, 2018[24]). In addition, the Superintendence of Finance (Superintendencia Financiera) is currently developing a green taxonomy to support financial actors and stakeholders across the public and private sectors. The taxonomy will incorporate a set of clear definitions to support the identification and evaluation of investments that can be considered as green or environmentally sustainable. A first series of documents under Phase 1 of the taxonomy development were released for public consultation[10] in September 2021.

These actions, amongst others, will be important to ensure there is a solid framework to enable green finance flows in support of Colombia's NDC and the government's wider environmental and sustainable development ambitions. Still, achieving these goals and targets set forth in policies such as the Green Growth and Bioeconomy strategies will require scaling up overall finance and investment in clean energy solutions, including measures to address the cost of debt for project development.

### *Tackling the cost of finance will support a stronger pipeline of bioenergy projects*

Currently, the cost of finance for bioenergy and other clean energy technologies can often be high, thereby limiting the pipeline of these projects. Part of this is due to limited experience with certain technologies, unfamiliarity with those types of projects and overall perceptions of risk by financial actors. Finance for some projects, including notably smaller transaction sizes (e.g. for rooftop PV and small biodigesters) can also be a challenge given the creditworthiness or lack of credit history of smaller borrowers. Difficulties in demonstrating clear revenue streams because of challenges in accessing long-term bilateral PPAs also play a hand in the cost of finance.

At the same time, the cost of finance is also influenced by the country's finance sector, which is controlled by a handful of fi nancial groups with low competition. This contributes to high interest rate margins (calculated as the difference between deposit and loan rates) that can exceed 7%, which is well above the margins observed in other Latin American countries like Chile and Mexico (OECD, 2019[26]). These high interest rate margins create subsequent challenges not only for generation projects but also for industries looking to invest in clean energy technologies (e.g. for on-site bioenergy capacity).

Strengthening financial regulation and encouraging greater competition in the banking sector can help to address the overall cost of finance in Colombia. A number of second tier banks in Colombia such as Bancoldex, Findeter and Finagro already offer concessional credit lines for bioenergy project development. This is equally the case for commercial banks such as Bancolombia, which provides a line for renewable energy investments for its agricultural and agro-industrial customers, with concessional finance under a leasing model (Box 4.3).

**Box 4.3. Arroz Federal rice husk gasification plant financed under a leasing model**

Arroz Federal, a ride producer located in Tolima in the centre-west of Colombia, invested in new bioenergy capacity in 2018 using rice husks as feedstock for power generation. The project, financed by Bancolombia, uses the husk by-product from the company's rice production which otherwise is disposed of as waste. Biogas is produced from the husks, which in turn is used to generate electricity through an internal combustion engine coupled to a generator.

The project, which became operational in 2019, is the first industrial-sized power generation plant using rice husks in Colombia. The new generation capacity is expected to produce around 2.2 gigawatt-hours of electricity output, resulting in a yearly reduction of about 450 tonnes of CO2 emissions. Additionally, the project will increase the mill's economic competitiveness by using available waste as direct feedstock for its energy needs. As Arroz Federal is grid connected, it could also potentially sell excess electricity to the grid, even if this is not currently envisaged for the project.

The facility investment was financed under a ten-year leasing model by Bancolombia for USD 772 million. Azimut Energía S.A.S., a company specialised in energy efficiency, implemented the project and is in charge of operating the system and guaranteeing that the energy production will meet Arroz Federal's annual consumption needs.

Bancolombia provided finance through its Leasing Agroverde line, which specialises in the modernisation of assets in the agricultural and agro-industrial sectors with objectives to improve productivity and environmental sustainability. While this type of project remains less common, the line of credit nevertheless provides attractive lending terms for energy efficiency and renewable energy projects as well as for sustainable construction and cleaner industrial production. It also provides technical advice on potential investments as needed and could be applied to similar bioenergy capacity installations.

Source: (Grupo Bancolombia, 2018[27]) (Grupo Bancolombia, 2021[28])

Still, many potential borrowers remain cautious of such investments, given the uncertainty and unfamiliarity with bioenergy technologies and their business models. Awareness raising and capacity building, such as the technical assistance offered by Bancolombia under its sustainable credit line to help borrowers to identify the appropriate technologies and relevant equipment suppliers should therefore be considered as a part of efforts to address access to finance and the overall cost of capital. Other support such as use of green credit facilities and targeted concessional lending can also encourage financing for bioenergy projects, particularly where borrowers or technologies are perceived as risky by private capital. For example, microfinance arrangements with local financial institutions can facilitate access to capital for small businesses or farmers looking to develop small on-site bioenergy solutions (Box 4.4).

### Box 4.4. Microfinance to improve access to clean energy finance in Bangladesh

The World Bank's Rural Electrification and Renewable Energy Development (RERED) programme used a combination of concessional credit and subsidies in Bangladesh to help develop a market for affordable clean energy solutions such as solar home systems, clean cookstoves and small bioenergy projects. Launched in 2008, the programme supported the installation of over one thousand solar irrigation pumps, 10 thousand domestic biogas digesters, 1.9 million improved cookstoves and 3.1 million solar home systems.

Finance for the RERED programme originated with the World Bank's International Development Association, which provided concessional credit with long-term maturity (38 years) to Bangladesh's Ministry of Finance. The World Bank equally acted as a conduit for grants from other parties, such as the Global Environment Facility, the Global Partnership on Output Based Aid and the Asian Development Bank. The Ministry of Finance then channelled these funds and concessional credit to Infrastructure Development Company Limited (IDCOL), a government-owned non-bank financial institution that implemented the programme. This included support through capacity building with local financial actors, such as microfinance institutions and technology providers, to increase capacity and improve familiarity with clean energy solutions. Local financial actors then helped to create demand for projects amongst their clients using tailored microfinance, such as purchase contracts and microcredit agreements.

A key part of the RERED programme was technical assistance to enable technology promotion and market development activities, alongside overall capacity for programme administration, monitoring and evaluation. Specifically, IDCOL provided training and capacity building to help partner organisations to develop technical expertise beyond their normal financial activities, which allowed them to become clean energy technology dealers (e.g. with technicians installing the technologies). A multi-layered monitoring and quality control process also helped to address issues in early stages of the programme.

Importantly, the RERED programme helped to overcome barriers such as access to affordable finance and low technical capacity in low-income markets. The targeted use of grants and concessional credit not only supported market development and de-risking activities but it also encouraged local financial institutions to take on projects previously considered as "non-productive loans". Economies of scale through the partnerships equally helped to bring down the cost of technology solutions in local markets, thereby improving the business case for lending. The overall success of the initiative was underscored by the entry of a number of private competitors outside the initiative, enabling market replication and attractive financing without support of the RERED programme.

Source: (World Bank, 2020[29]); (World Bank, 2014[30])

### *Public funds and blended finance can de-risk projects and leverage private capital*

Support can also be designed within or around existing funds and financial instruments. For instance, financing for local and municipal infrastructure projects under Territorial Development Finance (Financiera De Desarrollo Territorial, Findeter) could be used to support municipal waste-to-energy projects. Dedicated mechanisms (e.g. for biogas developments with industry) could similarly be designed within funds under the national development bank (Financiera de Desarrollo Nacional) or with the Ministry of Finance and Public Credit. Tools could likewise be designed in collaboration with banks such as Bancoldex or

Bancolombia, which already apply preferential interest rates under a leasing model for some clean energy projects, or with international development support.

While Colombia already has a number of national funds that are designed to support development of clean energy projects, these mostly provided support through grants. This limits the number of projects that can be supported and does not encourage active participation of private capital. Applying these funds more strategically (e.g. as tools for risk mitigation) will help to mobilise greater private investment and financing at improved rates. For example, FENOGE has a permanent source of capital through charges on electricity and has used this to support projects through grant-based schemes (GGGI, 2019[31]). Yet, the fund cannot currently lend to projects or invest in equity, which limits the scale of its activities. Widening the mandate to broaden FENOGE's activities for co-investment in clean energy projects with private sector engagement would help the fund to play a larger role in scaling up finance and investment in clean energy solutions, for instance by targeting the injection of public support to diminish perceived risk for technologies like anaerobic digestion technologies.

The national fund for the electrification of ZNI (Fondo de apoyo financiero para la energización de las zonas no interconectadas) and the financial support fund for inter-connected rural zones (Fondo de Apoyo Financiero para la Energización de las Zonas Rurales Interconectadas) similarly could be tailored to support the financing of bioenergy projects in ZNI and rural areas. De-risking tools such as guarantees and credit enhancement can help enable less-established renewable energy technologies and businesses to access private finance (OECD, 2021[32]). On-lending and co-lending structures can likewise increase the availability of attractive finance whilst helping local finance institutions to gain confidence in lending to renewable energy projects (IRENA, 2016[33]). For instance, the Clean Energy Finance Corporation of Australia uses aggregation partnerships with commercial banks throughout the country to offer debt (on-lending) for financing of eligible clean energy technologies.[11] This wholesale finance model offers low-cost funding to financial partners, who in turn can offer attractive terms such as discounted interest rates. As of 2019, these partnerships enabled over AUD 800 million (about USD 575 million) in investments in more than 5 500 small-scale projects (Wapner and Youngs, 2019[34]).

Colombia can also work with multilateral and international funds to design blended finance mechanisms that help to catalyse private finance for bioenergy projects. For example, the United Kingdom's Partnering for Accelerated Climate Transitions (UK PACT) Green Recovery Challenge Fund and the World Bank's Scale-up Climate Finance initiative both have targeted bioenergy as part of their support for clean energy development. A number of these global funds[12] could be leveraged to draw in private finance for bioenergy projects in Colombia through de-risking instruments like first loss and partial risk guarantees, co-investments and subordination, amongst others.[13] Blended finance mechanisms under the Ministry of Finance and Public Credit could be used to channel climate finance and development funds to bioenergy projects, possibly through the creation of a multi-donor blended finance platform such as the Indonesia One Fund (Box 4.5). Experiences with other dedicated green finance facilities such as those in Mongolia and South Africa equally highlight the role of different models that can be used to enable private investments in clean energy and crowd in private capital for projects that would not otherwise be financed by the market (OECD, 2021[8]).

**Box 4.5. Achieving Sustainable Development Goals (SDG) through the SDG Indonesia One Fund**

Indonesia has been an active contributor to the development of blended finance mechanisms that use development funds to help catalyse private finance. In 2018, the country's Ministry of Finance and the state-owned enterprise responsible for financing infrastructure projects in the country (PT Sarana Multi Infrastruktur, PT SMI) launched an integrated blended finance platform known as SDG Indonesia One. The initiative is a multi-donor blended finance platform with about USD 3 billion in funding commitments for supporting Indonesia's achievement of its SDGs. It is one of the first such initiatives globally, integrating multiple funding areas across the stages of project development, from project preparation and de-risking to financing and equity.

At the implementation level, PT SMI is responsible for managing the fund and working closely with development finance institutions in setting up a variety of financing facilities, including those dedicated to supporting clean energy development. These flexible financing products can include first loss instruments and partial risk guarantees, as well as co-investments and subordination. One notable example is the use of a grant from the French development bank Agence Française de Développement to set up a first-loss mechanism covering a maximum of 15% of the loan value for a mini-hydro plant. This helped to encourage other commercial banks to fund the project.

In effect, the SDG One Indonesia fund is designed to leverage donor funds to improve project bankability and crowd in private capital. For example, the platform's equity fund can be used to create opportunities for private capital to participate in greenfield and brownfield projects. This strategic use of blended finance will help to enable clean energy solutions in Indonesia, improving market viability and demonstrating the business opportunities and financing models for clean energy technologies.

Sources: (ADB, 2020[35]) and (PTSMI, 2021[36]).

### *Capital markets are an untapped opportunity for clean energy development*

Meeting the overall investment needs for Colombia's renewable energy ambitions, including bioenergy development, will also require increased availability of long-term capital, alongside further development of the country's capital market. The stock and bond markets in Colombia are both less developed than those in some regional peers, thereby missing the opportunity to shift savings from short-term deposits towards longer-term investments like clean energy development (OECD, 2019[17]). Recent green bond issuances, including Colombia's first sovereign green bond in September 2021 as well as green and sustainable bond issuances by Banco W and Icetex that were supported by Bancolombia, are encouraging signals of progress in engaging the financial sector and capital market to meet the country's sustainable development ambitions. Still, obstacles impede important opportunities to attract long-term finance for clean energy assets and investments.

In particular, the corporate bond market in Colombia remains underdeveloped compared to regional peers, namely due to low liquidity and financial sector issues, including higher costs of bond issuances than bank credits, few institutional investors and a highly regulated investment environment (OECD, 2019[17]). The result is that most bond issuance has been by the government and financial sector issuers (e.g. for green financial products) with little corporate green bond issuance (UNEPFI, 2020[37]). In fact, while Colombia was the second largest Latin American issuer of sovereign bonds in international debt markets for the first quarter of 2021, it was the second smallest issuer of international corporate bonds (UNECLAC, 2021[38]).

The capital market has likewise not been a significant source of funding for clean energy projects. There are only a few large companies comfortable with the costs and benefits of listing on the securities market, which is not uncommon in Latin America (OECD, 2019[26]). However, the Colombian equity market has noticeably lower liquidity levels compared to its peers, and in 2017, the average annual trading volume of the market represented only 4.2% of GDP (by comparison, Chile and México were 13.7% and 9.5%, respectively). Moreover, market capitalisation of domestic companies (39% of GDP in 2020, (World Bank, 2021[39])) also has moved towards consolidation and delisting among public companies: from 110 stock issuers in 2001 to 68 in 2019 (Reuters, 2019[40]). This is notably due to burdensome regulation, including listing and disclosure requirements, which drive up the cost of listing companies. This can be particularly dissuasive for small and medium enterprises (OECD, 2019[17]).

In response, the government created a Capital Market Mission (Misión Mercado de Capitales)[14] in late 2018, which subsequently identified critical barriers that have not allowed market development and provided a number of recommendations for future action in its final report in 2019. These suggested measures and reforms should support achievement of a deeper, more efficient capital market that can support more robust financing for clean energy projects and companies (e.g. by reducing the costs of access to the market). Additional measures, such as the emerging taxonomy framework, will also help to support capital flows towards green projects and clean energy development.

Building on these promising developments, the government can consider further policy and regulatory actions to help diversify financial products and develop capital market instruments for clean energy projects. These can be complemented by measures such as training and capacity building to familiarise market actors with the institutional and operational aspects of those projects. Standardisation of project documentation and measures to address issues of scale necessary to attract international capital (e.g. through support for aggregation and securitisation of projects) can develop use of debt market instruments, such as asset backed securities and sustainability-linked bonds. These instruments will help to deepen and expand the current investor base for clean energy development, for instance by tapping into international institutional investors such as insurance and pension funds.

Tapping into capital markets can also help to recycle capital for clean energy development, including possible refinancing at more attractive terms. Globally, institutional capital has shown a preference for operating assets (e.g. existing bioenergy cogeneration and hydropower capacity), as these typically have clear revenue streams and avoid investor risks in the design and development stages of a project. In fact, between 2009 and 2019, over 75% of global renewable energy deals involving institutional investors were in operating assets (IRENA, 2020[41]). Support for the early design and use of capital market instruments (e.g. possible application of a credit enhancement mechanism to help clean energy projects to achieve credit ratings of AA and above) can help to unlock access to these institutional markets, whilst generating interest in further developments by providing a clearer risk-return profile for investors.

## References


ABREN (2021), *Brazil opens path for Waste-to-Energy projects*, Brazilian Association for Energy Recovery of Waste (Associação Brasileira de Recuperação Energética de Resíduos, ABREN), https://abren.org.br/en/2021/01/14/brazil-opens-path-for-waste-to-energy-projects-bnamericas/ (accessed on 4 October 2021). [12]

ABREN (2020), *Ministry of Mines and Energy Announces Brazil's First MSW Energy Recovery Auction (MME Anuncia o Primeiro Leilão de Recuperação Energética de RSU do Brasil)*, Brazilian Association for Energy Recovery of Waste (Associação Brasileira de Recuperação Energética de Resíduos, ABREN), https://abren.org.br/en/2020/12/09/mme-anuncia-o-primeiro-leilao-de-recuperacao-energetica-de-rsu-do-brasil/ (accessed on 30 September 2021). [9]

ADB (2020), *Proposed Loan and Technical Assistance Grant Indonesia: Sustainable Development Goals Indonesia One-Green Finance Facility Phase 1*, Asian Development Bank (ADB), https://www.adb.org/projects/54152-001/main (accessed on 5 October 2021). [35]

BNAmericas (2021), *'Without thermal plants, we would already be rationing energy' - BNamericas*, Interviews, https://www.bnamericas.com/en/interviews/without-thermal-plants-we-would-already-be-rationing-energy (accessed on 5 October 2021). [16]

DNP (2018), "CONPES 3934", in *Green Growth Policy (Política de Crecimiento Verde)*, National Council for Social and Economic Policy (Consejo Nacional de Política Económica y Social, CONPES), National Planning Department (Departamento Nacional de Planeación, DNP), https://colaboracion.dnp.gov.co/CDT/Conpes/Econ%C3%B3micos/3934.pdf (accessed on 6 September 2021). [20]

Espejo, S. (2021), *Colombia accelerating reforms to attract investment in clean energy generation*, S&P Global - Platts, https://www.spglobal.com/platts/en/market-insights/latest-news/electric-power/030121-ceraweek-colombia-accelerating-reforms-to-attract-investment-in-clean-energy-generation (accessed on 28 September 2021). [3]

GGGI (2019), *Review of GGGI's Experience to Design and Operationalize National Financing Vehicles to Finance Climate and Green Growth Policy Implementation — Global Green Growth Institute*, Global Green Growth Institute, Seoul, https://gggi.org/report/review-of-gggis-experience-to-design-and-operationalize-national-financing-vehicles-to-finance-climate-and-green-growth-policy-implementation/ (accessed on 4 October 2021). [31]

Grupo Bancolombia (2021), *Leasing Agroverde*, Products and Services of Bancolombia, https://www.bancolombia.com/wps/portal/negocios/productos-financieros/leasing-agroverde (accessed on 29 November 2021). [28]

Grupo Bancolombia (2018), *Arroz Federal builds the first risk husk power generation plan in the country (1ra planta de generación de energía con cascarilla de arroz)*, Press Release, https://www.bancolombia.com/wps/portal/acerca-de/sala-prensa/noticias/innovacion/primera-planta-generacion-de-energia-con-cascarilla-de-arroz/!ut/p/z0/04_Sj9CPykssy0xPLMnMz0vMAfIjo8zijdwtPQ29TQz9DFz8XQ0CvZ18A42cTA0DQkz0C7IdFQEIXZOT (accessed on 29 November 2021). [27]

IFC (2018), *Country Progress Report: Addendum to SBN Global Progress Report - Colombia*, International Finance Corporation (IFC) Sustainable Banking Network, https://www.ifc.org/wps/wcm/connect/61248fe6-e9ba-4cb3-aed0-581e50e842e3/SBN+Country+Progress+Report+-+Colombia.pdf?MOD=AJPERES&CVID=m745XQC (accessed on 1 October 2021). [24]

InnoEnergy (2021), *Investment Round for Innovation Projects*, EIT Inno Energy, https://investmentround.innoenergy.com/ (accessed on 5 October 2021). [23]

InnoEnergy (2020), *EIT InnoEnergy Impact Report 2020*, Discover Innovative Solutions, https://www.innoenergy.com/discover-innovative-solutions/reports/impact-report-2020/ (accessed on 5 October 2021). [22]

IRENA (2020), *Renewable energy finance: Institutional capital*, International Renewable Energy Agency (IRENA), https://www.irena.org/publications/2020/Jan/RE-finance-Institutional-capital (accessed on 1 October 2021). [41]

IRENA (2016), *Unlocking Renewable Energy Investment: The role of risk mitigation and structured finance*, International Renewable Energy Agency (IRENA), https://www.irena.org/publications/2016/Jun/Unlocking-Renewable-Energy-Investment-The-role-of-risk-mitigation-and-structured-finance (accessed on 1 October 2021). [33]

IRENA and USAID (2021), *Renewable energy auctions in Colombia: context, design and results*, International Renewable Energy Agency (IRENA) and United States Agency for International Development (USAID), https://www.irena.org/publications/2021/March/Renewable-energy-auctions-in-Colombia. [7]

Lim, W., E. Yuen and A. Bhaskar (2021), "Waste-to-energy: Green solutions for emerging markets", *KPMG*, https://home.kpmg/xx/en/home/insights/2019/10/waste-to-energy-green-solutions-for-emerging-markets.html (accessed on 30 September 2021). [10]

Morganstein, J. et al. (2021), "Renewable Energy Procurement Guidebook for Colombia", *World Resources Institute*, http://dx.doi.org/10.46830/WRIGB.19.00129. [4]

OECD (2021), *Clean Energy Finance and Investment Policy Review of Indonesia*, Green Finance and Investment, OECD Publishing, Paris, https://dx.doi.org/10.1787/0007dd9d-en. [8]

OECD (2021), *Global experience in catalysing renewable energy finance and investment*, Organisation for Economic Co-operation and Development (OECD), https://www.oecd.org/cefim/india/global-study/ (accessed on 1 October 2021). [32]

OECD (2021), *OECD International Direct Investment Statistics*, Organisation for Economic Co-operation and Development (OECD), https://dx.doi.org/10.1787/2307437x. [5]

OECD (2020), *Agricultural Policy Monitoring and Evaluation 2020*, OECD Publishing, Paris, https://dx.doi.org/10.1787/928181a8-en. [18]

OECD (2020), *Research and Development Statistics 2020*, Organisation for Economic Co-operation and Development (OECD), Paris, https://www.oecd.org/sti/inno/researchanddevelopmentstatisticsrds.htm (accessed on 1 October 2021). [21]

OECD (2019), *Equity Market Development in Latin America: Colombia*, Organisation for Economic Co-operation and Development (OECD), https://www.oecd.org/corporate/ca/Colombia-Latin-America-Equity-Markets.pdf (accessed on 30 September 2021). [26]

OECD (2019), *OECD Economic Surveys: Colombia 2019*, OECD Publishing, Paris, https://dx.doi.org/10.1787/e4c64889-en. [17]

OECD (2014), *OECD Review of Innovation Policy: Colombia*, OECD, Paris. [19]

PTSMI (2021), *SDG Indonesia One*, Strategic Operation, https://ptsmi.co.id/sdg-indonesia-one (accessed on 5 October 2021). [36]

REGlobal (2021), *Brazil sets ceiling price for upcoming A-5 auction*, News -Analysis and perspectives for CXOs, https://reglobal.co/brazil-sets-ceiling-price-for-upcoming-a-5-auction/ (accessed on 4 October 2021). [13]

Renewables Now (2021), *Brazil registers 437 MW of renewables for capacity reserve auction*, News, https://renewablesnow.com/news/brazil-registers-437-mw-of-renewables-for-capacity-reserve-auction-754132/ (accessed on 5 October 2021). [15]

Renewables Now (2021), *Contracts awarded to 861 MW of renewables in Brazil's latest tender*, News, https://renewablesnow.com/news/contracts-awarded-to-861-mw-of-renewables-in-brazils-latest-tender-755961/ (accessed on 5 October 2021). [14]

Reuters (2019), *Reforms to Colombia capital market may face rough road in Congress: experts*, https://www.reuters.com/article/us-colombia-economy-idINKCN1VB2CB (accessed on 1 October 2021). [40]

RVO (2021), *Waste Management in the LATAM Region: Business Opportunities for the Netherlands in waste/circular economy sector in eight countries of Latin America*, The Netherlands Enterprise Agency (RVO), https://www.rvo.nl/sites/default/files/2021/02/Report_LATAM_Waste_Management_feb_2021.pdf (accessed on 16 September 2021). [11]

Schwab, K. (2019), *Insight Report: The Global Competitiveness Report 2019*, World Economic Forum, Geneva, http://www3.weforum.org/docs/WEF_TheGlobalCompetitivenessReport2019.pdf (accessed on 28 September 2021). [1]

Schwab, K. (2010), *The Global Competitiveness Report 2010-2011*, World Economic Forum, Geneva, http://www3.weforum.org/docs/WEF_GlobalCompetitivenessReport_2010-11.pdf (accessed on 28 September 2021). [2]

UNECLAC (2021), *Capital Flows to Latin America and the Caribbean: first four months of 2021*, United Nations Economic Commission for Latin America and the Caribbean (UNECLAC), Santiago, https://www.cepal.org/sites/default/files/news/files/capital_flows_to_lac_first_four_months_of_2021.pdf (accessed on 8 October 2021). [38]

UNEP (2021), *Sustainable Finance Activities in Latin America & the Caribbean*, United Nations Environment Programme (UNEP) Finance Initiative, https://www.unepfi.org/wordpress/wp-content/uploads/2021/06/Country-Profiles-Sustainable-Finance-Activities-Somente-Leitura.pdf (accessed on 1 October 2021). [25]

UNEPFI (2020), *COLOMBIA - Sustainable Finance Activities*, UNEP Finance Initiative. [37]

Wapner, A. and R. Youngs (2019), *Green Bank Insight: Aggregation and Securitization*, Coalition for Green Capital, https://greenbanknetwork.org/wp-content/uploads/2019/04/Green-Bank-Aggregation-and-Securitization-Coalition-for-Green-Capital.pdf (accessed on 1 October 2021). [34]

World Bank (2021), *Market capitalization of listed domestic companies (% of GDP)*, World Federation of Exchanges Database, https://data.worldbank.org/indicator/CM.MKT.LCAP.GD.ZS (accessed on 1 October 2021). [39]

World Bank (2020), *Rural Electrification and Renewable Energy Development II (RERED II) Project (P131263)*, Implementation Status & Results Report, https://documents1.worldbank.org/curated/en/288301608727922563/pdf/Disclosable-Version-of-the-ISR-Rural-Electrification-and-Renewable-Energy-Development-II-RERED-II-Project-P131263-Sequence-No-39.pdf (accessed on 5 October 2021). [29]

World Bank (2019), *Learning from Developing Country Power Market Experiences : The Case of Colombia*, World Bank Group, Washington DC, https://documents.worldbank.org/en/publication/documents-reports/documentdetail/898231552316685139/learning-from-developing-country-power-market-experiences-the-case-of-colombia (accessed on 27 August 2021). [6]

World Bank (2014), *Scaling Up Access to Electricity: The Case of Bangladesh*, https://documents1.worldbank.org/curated/en/699721468003918010/pdf/88702-REPF-BRI-PUBLIC-Box385194B-ADD-SERIES-Live-wire-knowledge-note-series-LW21-New-a-OKR.pdf (accessed on 5 October 2021). [30]

## Notes

[1] For more information, see: https://thelawreviews.co.uk/title/the-public-competition-enforcement-review/colombia.

[2] For more information (in Spanish), see: https://gestornormativo.creg.gov.co/gestor/entorno/docs/resolucion_creg_0131_1998.htm.

[3] For more information (in Spanish), see: https://www.mincit.gov.co/minindustria/competitividad-e-innovacion.

[4] For more information (in Spanish), see: http://www.colombiacompetitiva.gov.co/snci/el-sistema/comision-nacional-competitividad-innovacion.

[5] More information: https://www.innoenergy.com/about/about-eit-innoenergy/eit-at-a-glance/.

[6] For more information (in Spanish), see: https://www.asobancaria.com/2016/02/01/guias/.

[7] For more information (in Spanish), see: https://www.asobancaria.com/wp-content/uploads/2017/01/V2-Gui%CC%81a-General-de-Implementacio%CC%81n-ARAS-12-Ene-2107-1.pdf.

[8] For more information, see: https://climate-laws.org/geographies/colombia/policies/national-climate-change-decree-sisclima.

[9] For more information, see: https://cdkn.org/wp-content/uploads/2017/07/Roadmap-actions-for-setting-a-green-bond-market-in-Colombia.pdf.

[10] For more information (in Spanish), see: https://www.superfinanciera.gov.co/jsp/10109182.

[11] For more information, see: https://www.oecd.org/cefim/india/CEFC/.

[12] For more information, see: http://www.globalbioenergy.org/fileadmin/user_upload/gbep/docs/Financing_tool/Funding_Instruments_for_Bioenergy_Projects_and_Programmes_2021_UPDATE.pdf.

[13] For more information, see: OECD Progress update on Approaches to Mobilising Institutional investment for Sustainable Infrastructure.

[14] For more information (in Spanish), see: http://www.urf.gov.co/webcenter/portal/urf/pages_c/misinmercadodecapitales.

# 5 Insights for enabling greater finance and investment for bioenergy solutions

Policy reforms and market signals have played a critical role in enabling clean energy development in Colombia, such as recent solar and wind additions. Unlocking opportunities for bioenergy requires building upon this progress to target regulatory measures and market incentives that enable finance and investment in these solutions. The government of Colombia can take a number of actions such as establishing clear targets and capacity additions, improving co-ordination across relevant authorities, strengthening guidance and regulations on waste disposal, and ensuring access to the grid for distributed energy solutions. The government can also work with partners to improve awareness and familiarity with bioenergy technologies, whilst also supporting targeted financial schemes to encourage affordable finance and de-risk investment in those projects.

Colombia has made remarkable progress over the last decade in developing the overall policy environment and market framework for clean energy development. The government's recent Nationally Determined Contribution (NDC) update, alongside a number of important high-level policy signals like the Green Growth, Circular Economy and Bioeconomy strategies, have all emphasised the country's commitment to reducing its greenhouse gas emissions and achieving its Sustainable Development Goals. Further reforms, such as on-going capital market improvements and the emerging sustainable finance framework through the forthcoming taxonomy, are also critical measures signalling the government's intent to achieve these high-level sustainability ambitions.

Still, enabling the clean energy transition through opportunities like bioenergy development requires additional policy signals, regulatory reforms and market incentives to create the enabling environment for investment in these solutions. Colombia is fortunate to have considerable clean energy resources, from outstanding solar and wind capacities to untapped agricultural, industrial and municipal waste streams that can be used to produce multiple forms of bioenergy, whether these be biofuels for transport, biogas for industry or biodigestion for clean electricity and heat production. These bioenergy opportunities can play a critical role in addressing growing reliance on fossil fuel imports, not only tapping into domestically available renewable energy resources but also increasing security of supply through local energy sources, for instance for small-scale electricity generation in areas not connected to the national grid.

Recent developments such as the 2019 renewable energy auctions have drawn interest from both national and international developers and investors, signalling the significant opportunity to achieve clean energy ambitions with private sector participation. However, opening the door for scaled-up private capital for finance and investment of clean energy development requires additional targeted measures that ensure a robust pipeline of bankable projects. This includes clear reflection of NDCs and sustainable development ambitions in national energy policy, notably signalling the expected role of clean energy, including bioenergy vectors, with respect to fossil fuel use in the country's short-, medium- and long-term development strategies. Critically, this will create the policy environment for project developers, businesses and investors to formulate their own strategic plans on actions forward.

Policy signals can also more clearly address the expected roles and opportunities for bioenergy projects including how they link to the achievement of multiple national ambitions, ranging from secure, reliable and affordable energy to better waste management, improved productivity and enhanced bioecology. Lessons extracted from experiences with bioenergy technology use and growth in the sugarcane and palm oil industries can help to design the appropriate policy tools, regulatory measures, market incentives and financial support to drive uptake of these technologies in other applications.

This includes opportunities for bioenergy use for electricity generation, which in addition to providing more secure and reliable local clean energy capacity, for instance in non-interconnected zones (zonas no interconectadas ZNI), can also help to phase-down fossil fuel use in power generation, address the increasing impact of climate effects on the country's formidable hydroelectricity capacity and help to close the gap to meet the National governments' ambition to have 100% energy access by 2030. Bioenergy capacity also can support further deployment of variable renewable electricity sources such as solar and wind, playing an important role across the wholesale, firm (reliability) and spot markets.

Yet, these values need to be more clearly reflected in energy market policy, regulations and electricity market design. Specifically, Planning Unit of the Ministry of Mines and Energy (Unidad de Planeación Minero Energética, UPME) electricity generation plans do not sufficiently reflect the strategic value of bioenergy solutions given the heavy reliance on the current pipeline of planned capacity additions, which effectively benefits incumbent technologies over new and emerging ones. Rules around electricity market access (e.g. for off-site power purchase agreements with unregulated customers) and the consequences of a considerably integrated market, compelling high dependence on retailer willingness to connect distributed generation projects, also make for critical barriers to bioenergy electricity capacity additions.

Renewable energy portfolio standards, without retailer benefit to work with self-generators, cogenerators and unregulated consumers, likewise limit opportunities for bioenergy projects.

The regulatory environment for waste management, which does not sufficiently encourage sorting, treatment, recycling, re-use and recovery of waste, further compounds the challenges for bioenergy development. While Colombia has a strong framework for waste collection and disposal, landfill fees are quite low and despite calls to reduce waste streams, there is no legally binding framework to encourage development of alternatives to disposal. The number of actors, authorities and regulations touching on waste-to-energy opportunities also make it challenging to navigate development of such applications.

Access to finance is another key barrier to bioenergy projects. While green finance flows may be improving, including notably for large, utility-scale renewable energy development, the cost of finance for bioenergy and other less established clean energy technologies is still typically high, limiting the overall pipeline of these projects. Limited experience with bioenergy technologies, unfamiliarity with their application and the creditworthiness (or lack of credit history) of smaller borrowers increase the overall perceptions of risk to investors. Even more established applications, such as sugar-cane bioenergy co-generation, often rely on existing corporate credit lines, which can add to the cost of finance for capacity additions.

To address these issues, the government of Colombia can take a number of actions to improve the overall conditions for bioenergy finance and investment. These include:

- Establishing clear targets for bioenergy and other clean energy capacity additions within UPME's Reference Electricity Expansion Plans, reflecting national policy priorities for the country's energy transition and the techno-economic potential of these technologies to meet Colombia's strategic policy ambitions.
- Improving institutional co-ordination across the relevant authorities and related policies that influence opportunities to develop bioenergy capacity. Such co-ordination could be led by the National Planning Department (Departamento Nacional de Planeación), or the government could consider the creation of a specific task force of co-ordinating body to manage inter-sectoral public and economic policy touching on bioenergy development, like the Inter-institutional Bioenergy Table in Ecuador.
- Strengthening opportunities for waste-to-energy projects through clear policy guidance and strengthened market signals such as increased gate fees for landfills and more stringent extended producer responsibility measures, including possible mandatory end-of-life requirements for manufacturers and industry. The Ministry of Environment and Sustainable Development (Ministerio de Ambiente y Desarrollo Sostenible) and Ministry of Mines and Energy (Ministerio de Minas y Energía, MME), in co-operation with other authorities such as the Ministry of Housing, City and Territory, can also provide support for innovative business models to sort, treat and recover waste, including for energy production.
- Ensuring fair and non-discriminatory access to the grid, reviewing current market practices to address barriers under 2018 reforms that still limit development of bioenergy opportunities, for instance through bilateral contracts for corporate sourcing of renewables. As part of this review, the Energy and Gas Regulation Commission (Comisión de Regulación de Energía y Gas, CREG) can provide clearer guidance and eventual regulatory measures to enable better power wheeling arrangements to facilitate businesses (whether unregulated or regulated customers) that would seek procurement of off-site bioelectricity production.
- Working with domestic stakeholders like the National Centre for Cleaner Production and Environmental Technology (Centro Nacional de Producción Más Limpia y Tecnologías Ambientales) to build awareness and capacity for bioenergy development. This includes engaging industry familiar with market needs and opportunities for bioenergy projects, as has been the case with the sugar association, Asocaña. Similar industry groups, like the National Fund for Pork

Producers, Porkcolombia, can help sector actors to navigate regulations and the project approval and permitting processes, whilst helping to identify ways to streamline procedures to reduce administrative costs and timelines for biogas development.

- Assessing opportunities to implement targeted financial schemes to increase flows of capital to bioenergy projects, including development of tools such as guarantees, green credit facilities and concessional lending that enable more attractive finance and diminish perceived risks for investors. These support mechanisms and transaction enablers can be designed within existing funds and facilities, such as Findeter and FENOGE, and/or in partnership with international funds or climate finance (e.g. through blended finance) to maximise use of public funds in a way that catalyses private investment in bioenergy development.
- Pursuing continued capital market reforms with further policy and regulatory actions such standardisation of project documentation to help diversify financial products and develop market instruments such as green bonds that can attract capital for clean energy projects at the necessary scales. This include co-operation across relevant authorities such MME and the Ministry of Finance and Public Credit to carry out training and capacity building that familiarises market actors with the institutional and operational aspects of bioenergy and other clean energy projects.

In addition, MME can work with key partners like UPME to improve information on the business case and market opportunities for bioenergy development. This could include developing a bioenergy project or mapping database, similar to the Australian Renewable Energy Mapping Infrastructure[1] and Indonesia Geoportal One Map[2] to provide data and information on bioenergy resource potential with respect to existing and planned transmission and distribution capacity. This could include other dynamic information, such as electricity demand profiles and local electricity and energy prices, and could be tied to investment promotion under the ProColombia portal.

Given that bioenergy technologies can struggle to compete with the falling cost of solar and wind projects, MME and CREG can also consider targeted measures to support bioenergy market development over the next decade, in line with the technical potential and policy priorities highlighted in the Green Growth, Circular Economy and Bioeconomy strategies. Such measures can include targeted procurement of bioenergy capacity additions outside future renewable energy auctions as well as designing features within the auctions to support participation of bioenergy solutions. This could be through tailored support such as government guarantees of certain types of bioenergy projects to address barriers to participation, like the required performance bonds and start-up guarantees. Future auction design could also include pricing that incorporates elements like a locational component, which has been used in Mexico to help select projects over other less expensive ones if they had more value for the system.

Other targeted support, such as design of possible public-private partnership (PPP) models for bioenergy projects, will likewise encourage greater input of private capital for bioenergy technology development, whilst carrying public resources further. These PPP structures could initially target bioenergy technologies that have a wide potential across the economy or be designed strategically to attract capital to bioenergy projects of strategic interest, for instance in ZNI.

Lastly, public support can target new bioenergy applications, technologies and business models through clean energy incubators and other innovation support schemes. These can help develop bioenergy solutions and market models fit for the Colombian context, whilst enabling greater national expertise in bioenergy capacity development and increasing productivity across important economic sectors like industry and agriculture.

## Notes

[1] For more information, see: https://arena.gov.au/projects/aremi-project/.

[2] For more information, see: https://geoportal.esdm.go.id/monaresia/home/.

# Annex A. Global experiences with bioenergy development

Bioenergy solutions, including waste-to-energy applications, make up a diverse landscape of technologies and feedstocks that can be used for heat and power generation, amongst other uses like biofuels for transport. Abundant residues in Colombia, from livestock and agriculture as well as municipal and industrial waste can be used to meet the country's clean energy ambitions, alongside other socioeconomic and environmental goals such as reduced emissions and limiting waste going to landfills. Bioenergy solutions, like the current use of waste residues for energy generation in Colombia's sugarcane and palm industries, can address heavy reliance on fossil fuels and the country's growing dependence on energy imports. Tapping into locally available waste can equally support ambitions to provide clean, reliable and affordable energy, for instance in zones not connected to the national grid. Yet, unlocking opportunities for these solutions will require co-ordinated action to create the enabling environment for bioenergy finance and investment.

The following case studies consider international practice in supporting the development of emerging bioenergy and waste-to-energy markets. In particular, these examples assess the policy considerations and support mechanisms that helped to create an enabling environment for finance and investment in those projects, from both domestic and international sources. Lessons learned from the experiences in Brazil, Chile, India, Turkey and even domestically in Colombia shine light on the different policy measures and good practices that can be applied in Colombia to scale up finance and investment in bioenergy applications.

## Brazil: from waste to energy in the cement industry

Cement production is one of the most energy-intensive industries in the world, given the required crushing, grinding and blending of raw materials (mainly limestone and clay) that are burned at high temperatures (around 1 450 degrees Celsius) in a kiln in order to produce clinker, which is afterwards ground with gypsum to produce the final cement product. Fossil fuels, including in particular petroleum coke (petcoke), are consequently a major input into cement manufacturing, and the average amount of tonnes of $CO_2$ released per tonne of cement produced has continued to increase globally over the last decade (IEA, 2021[1]).

Given the high-heat consumption and energy intensity (e.g. for grinding) of the cement production process, energy-related expenses can account for as much as 30-40% of cement companies' operating costs (IFC, 2017[2]). The global cement industry subsequently started looking as early as the 1970s for substitutes to fossil fuels in order to reduce cash costs and to improve economic competitiveness. Since then, there has also been greater attention paid to the environmental impact of cement production, and finding economically viable alternative fuel solutions, without reducing the quality of cement, has become a central strategy to mitigating the carbon footprint of the sector.

In Brazil, the cement industry has one of the lowest $CO_2$ intensities in the world, thanks to a number of actions that the sector has taken since the 1990s, including for example energy efficiency measures and clinker substitution. While overall cement production in the country grew by nearly 275% between 1990 and 2014, the sector's emissions intensity dropped by 18% over the period, from 700 to 564 kilogrammes of $CO_2$ per tonne (SNIC, 2019[3]). This reduction was due in part to the use of alternative fuels, which began to grow in earnest in the early 2000s due to concerns about fluctuations in petcoke prices. By 2014, 14% of energy used for cement manufacturing in the country was through co-processing with alternative fuels, and this share has continued to grow, reaching about 30% in 2020 (ABCP, 2021[4]).

### *Alternative fuel use for cement production in Brazil*

Co-processing in the country's cement sector began in the early 1990s when Votorantim Cimentos, the largest cement producer in Brazil, completed its first demonstration of alternative fuel inputs using industrial waste at one of its plants in Paraná in the south of the country. Since then, alternative fuels such as tyres, agricultural residues (e.g. rice husks and açai pits) and industrial waste have become more common for co-processing across the cement industry. For example, 14 of Votorantim's plants in Brazil co-process waste to substitute part of the petcoke used in kilns with alternative fuels (Cemnet, 2020[5]).

A wide variety of alternative fuels can be used for co-processing in cement plants, ranging from biomass and municipal waste to sludge, tyres and even hazardous industrial waste such as spent solvents and used oil. The type of alternative fuel determines its thermal substitution value and pre-treatment may be necessary with some refuse-derived fuel (RDF) in order to remove unwanted elements, increase the calorific value and/or convert the fuel input into forms compatible with the cement kiln.

Tyres and hazardous industrial waste are the most common alternative fuels used for cement co-processing in Brazil, in part due to their heat values and their availability. Other substitutes such as biomass and agricultural waste are also used, although they have a lower heating value and are used by other industries (e.g. biorefineries). Availability and cost of alternative fuels naturally influence their potential attractiveness for co-processing in cement production, where sufficient quality, density and predictability of RDF supply below petcoke prices has played an important role in justifying investments (e.g. for pre-processing and treatment capacity). Broadly speaking, cement companies in Brazil have typically looked to substitute petcoke with investments that have a payback less than three to five years (ABCP, 2021[4]).

A number of additional factors have influenced the use of alternative fuels in the country's cement sector. For instance, national regulations preventing tyres from going to landfills played a critical role in driving RDF use. Specifically, regulations set in 1999, then updated under National Council for the Environment (Conselho Nacional do Meio Ambiente, CONAMA) Resolution 416 of 2009, required manufacturers and importers to collect and dispose of old tyres for each new one produced. The National Tyre Industry Association (Associação Nacional da Indústria de Pneumáticos) accordingly worked to establish services for collection and final disposal of scrap tyres (da Silva, Chaves S. G. Francisco and Lopes, 2017[6]). This led to the creation of more than 1 500 collection points across the country, which supported development of waste and energy-recovery processes such as tyre granulation and co-processing in cement production.

Environmental sustainability has also played a role in co-processing in the cement sector. Already in 1999, Votorantim joined with the nine other largest cement manufacturers in the world to create the Cement Sustainability Initiative,[1] which set targets to mitigate the sector's environmental impact. In 2019, Brazil's National Union of Cement Industry (Sindicato Nacional da Indústria do Cimento, SNIC) and the Brazilian Portland Cement Association (Associação Brasileira de Cimento Portland, ABCP) launched a *Cement Technology Roadmap* with the Initiative, the International Energy Agency and the International Finance Corporation (SNIC, 2019[3]). This set further ambitions to reduce the specific $CO_2$ emissions from cement production in the country by another 14% over 2014 levels by 2030, increasing that target to 30% reductions by 2050. To achieve these ambitions, the roadmap noted the role of increasing alternative fuel use in line with the National Policy of Solid Waste (Política Nacional de Resíduos Sólidos, PNRS), setting targets to achieve 35% thermal substitution in cement production by 2030 and 55% by 2050.

PNRS was launched in 2010 by the federal government under Law No. 12.305,[2] which instituted national regulation on the reduction, re-utilisation, recycling, treatment and appropriate disposal of solid waste. Enforcement of this law has been more challenging compared to the tyre industry (which is a smaller pool of actors), but even so, it offers opportunity for further co-processing, given the roughly 79 million tonnes of urban waste generated annually in Brazil (Souza, 2019[7]). In fact, a first demonstration for municipal solid waste (MSW) co-processing was tested for licensing at Votorantim's Salto de Pirapora plant in São Paulo in 2018. Upgrades to the plant, including equipment modernisation and adaptation for co-processing, cost roughly USD 9 million (BRL 47 million) between 2016 and 2019, and the facility received a permanent environmental license to use MSW in 2019 after successful testing with nearly 18 thousand tonnes of RDF, resulting in 5.3% petcoke substitution (Votorantim, 2019[8]). Looking forward, Votorantim plans another USD 32 million (BRL 167 million) in investment for the plant to process up to 65 thousand tonnes of MSW per year. Four additional Votorantim plants are also adding capacity to transform collectively around 130 thousand tonnes of MSW to energy for cement production.

Under the SNIC Roadmap, the cement industry also set a voluntary target to increase use of MSW co-processing from almost nothing in 2019 to nearly 10% of fuel input by 2030, representing about 2.5 million tonnes of RDF for the sector (SNIC, 2019[3]). This initiative is being driven by industry considerations to tap into the large potential for MSW as a cost-effective solution beyond tyres and industrial waste. While the financial margin with respect to MSW cost and energy content is likely smaller than with tyres and hazardous industrial waste, cement manufacturers nevertheless consider that there is longer-term value in meeting sustainability targets and overall capacity to manage fluctuations in petcoke prices.

To achieve these ambitions, ensuring cost-effective supply and processing of MSW for cement co-processing will be critical. As in many other countries, MSW in Brazil is not only an environmental challenge but also often a waste management problem. Around 45% of municipal waste currently goes to landfills with no associated charges, and as much as 41% of MSW is not sent to appropriate sanitary waste sites (Gutberlet, Bramryd and Johansson, 2020[9]). Thus, while urban waste is an RDF opportunity for cement production, cost can still be an issue (as it is cheaper or free to landfill), and there can be little incentive to handle MSW for alternative uses.

Previous RDF experience with tyre co-processing (where roughly half of tyre waste, or 60 million tonnes per year, now goes to the cement industry) is helping in the development of an MSW market for cement production. For example, a pre-treatment facility was built by four companies that associated themselves to ensure sufficient, quality supply of RDF. A new MSW pre-treatment facility, Ecoparque Pernambuco, was also developed in 2019 to supply a LafargeHolcim cement plant located in Caaporã in the northeast of Brazil. ABCP has equally met with cement manufacturers in seven regions, representing roughly half of current co-processing capacity (1.2 million tonnes) in order to try to develop a cluster project for MSW.

The aim of these efforts is to promote co-operation with local governments in order to build a pipeline for MSW use in local cement industries. ABCP and its industry members are working with the Ministry of Environment to this extent in order to create an association with the two main waste groups in Brazil and increase potential synergies. Votorantim Cimentos also launched its own subsidiary, Verdera, in 2019 to provide waste management services across the country. This company is part of an overall transformational strategy for Votorantim, but it also builds upon opportunity to complement the company's main cement production activities and increase capacity for co-processing through waste management.

### *Policy measures to enable co-processing in cement production*

While cement co-processing in Brazil has been largely driven by industry initiative, it has been supported all the same by a policy framework creating the underlying, enabling conditions for RDF use. Importantly, CONAMA Resolution 264/1999[3] defined and approved waste incineration in cement kilns. Further regulation under CONAMA Resolution 316 of 2002[4] addressed thermal treatment of waste incineration with emission limits for dioxins and furans in co-processing.

The 2010 PNRS also provided impetus for co-processing, signalling the government's intent to end irregular landfills and illegal dumping, while also setting a legal hierarchy for waste management. While implementation of the PNRS encountered a number of challenges, including notably enforcement of local and federal waste disposal regulations, the federal government has worked to improve this situation and passed a new Basic Sanitation Framework under Federal Law No. 14.026 of 2020.[5] In addition to a number of important reforms (e.g. on public concession of sanitation and waters services), the law allows municipalities to begin charging a tax for waste management services. It also requires states to define their municipal waste management programmes. Additional measures included plans for an auction of electrical energy from MSW to improve the economic viability of alternative waste management and the government has also provided around USD 20 million in support to municipalities aiming to find solutions for better waste management, including industry co-processing (Government of Brazil, 2021[10]).

Additionally, Resolution 499 of 2020[6] replaced and updated the 1999 co-processing regulation with clearer procedures for licensing of waste burning in rotary kilns. This update pulled from European regulations, notably on emissions parameters and concentration limits of persistent organic pollutants in the composition of waste. It is now being implemented by individual states, which have autonomy to create their own regulations at the same level or better than federal requirements. One such example is in São Paulo, whose regulation for blending stations does not allow certain types of wastes (e.g. wood containing halogenated organic compounds) that are permitted (or are not explicitly excluded) elsewhere. São Paulo likewise has specific regulation on thermal treatment of MSW, noting explicit guidelines on licensing, operational conditions, emissions limits and monitoring criteria. In other instances, states have specific minimum heat values for alternative fuels in co-processing. For example, the state of Minas Gerais in south-eastern Brazil specifically mentions "treated household waste" at a minimum lower heating value of at least 6.3 gigajoules per tonne (Lima Cortez and Goldemberg, 2016[11]).

In some instances, these types of state guidelines can encourage MSW and other RDF co-processing, but the heterogeneity of policies, and specifically state regulations that prohibit or complicate co-processing of certain wastes allowed in other areas, was highlighted in the SNIC Roadmap as an important challenge to further implementation of alternative fuel use in the country's cement industry. Alternative fuels were equally highlighted as one of the three core pillars (alongside energy efficiency and clinker substitution) to decarbonise energy use in the cement sector and the roadmap highlighted recommendations to enable co-processing solutions moving forward. This included the suggestion to establish standardised procedures across the waste management chain in order to document, monitor and track waste. This could build upon current issuance of "thermal destruction certificates" for certain types of waste as regulated by CONAMA Resolution 316 of 2002. The roadmap also recommended expanding existing state regulations for MSW co-processing to set national standards for urban solid waste treatment and energy recovery.

SNIC, ABCP and others are now working with national and regional authorities, including the Ministry of Environment, to carry forward these recommendations and to improve the business case for alternative fuel use in Brazil's cement industry. A technical agreement was signed in 2020, and the first output was an atlas (Atlas de Recuperação Energética) showing the current status of energy recovery, including the potential for the future.

### *Lessons learned and implications for the Colombian context*

Experience with co-processing in Brazil's cement sector highlights that the success of alternative fuel use in industry depends on several important factors. This includes a well-defined regulatory framework for RDF use as well as an effective, reliable management process to ensure economically viable supply of waste. For example, manufacturer mandates for product recovery and disposal were critical to early adoption of cement co-processing with tyres. Policy guidelines and legal definitions on the use of residues in cement kilns also played a vital role in enabling industry investment, whilst measures such as the government's 2020 policy reforms have helped to facilitate licencing and industry participation. More recent efforts to expand co-processing to MSW substantiate this critical juxtaposition of waste management policy with industry regulation. Without levers to establish reliable MSW supply with consistent operational rules for manufacturers, there is low incentive to make long-term investments for alternative fuel use.

Colombia can learn from Brazil's experiences to promote similar opportunities for industry co-processing through waste-to-energy solutions. Co-processing may be recognised as a sustainable alternative under Ministry of Environment and Sustainable Development (Ministerio de Ambiente y Desarrollo Sostenible, MADS) Resolution 909 of 2008, but RDF use outside Colombia's sugar and palm industries remains limited. This is due in part to waste management and supply issues, where low tipping fees and lack of sorting and treatment do not facilitate development of co-processing capacity. Efforts to address these issues, such as the recently announced landfill tax, will help to address these barriers, although the Ministry of Mines and Energy (Ministerio de Minas y Energía, MME) and other relevant authorities should identify where more targeted policy support will enable industry initiative. For instance, the cement company Argos installed co-processing capacity using tyres as RDF at its Cartagena plant, using more than 75 thousand tonnes of waste as alternative fuel in 2018 (Stewardson, 2019[12]). This experience can provide useful insights for development of similar installations at other industry sites, highlighting where policy action can increase the opportunity and business case for co-processing.

One such action can be to encourage an early, clear supply chain of available refuse with good thermal substitution value, for instance by mandating extended producer responsibility requirements for tyre manufacturers, as was done in Brazil. Lessons from Brazil's cement sector and on-going efforts to expand RDF use to MSW stress this need for adequate waste management policy and disposal fees to ensure cost-effective fuel substitutes for petcoke. Industry concerns for environmental impact, consumer image and long-term decarbonisation may be factors that influence co-processing opportunities, but broadly speaking, these considerations still require a clear business case for RDF use (e.g. who will pay for pre-treatment of waste). This is underscored by low uptake of RDF in Colombia's cement sector, which like Brazil has concerns about petcoke price fluctuations but still has not actively pursued waste-to-energy opportunities.

Lessons can also be drawn on the impact of dialogue and co-ordination between industry and government. Brazil has benefited from leadership from SNIC and ABCP, who have supported co-ordination across stakeholders on matters relating to co-processing. Importantly, these associations provide a forum for cement manufacturers to engage with government, highlighting experiences and issues as well as actions to increase use of alternative fuels. These considerations can be pulled into the Colombian context, for instance through dialogues with the Latin American cement association (Federación Interamericana del Cemento) and the Colombia cement association, Procemco.

Brazil's experience highlights that working across such stakeholders (including actors such as landfill managers, recycling companies and municipal authorities) promotes an enabling environment for alternative fuel use in industry. Individual firms may be able to create "pocket" co-processing (i.e. local examples of supply and demand capacity), but achieving high shares of RDF use requires strong co-ordination of the actors and policies that influence the overall waste-to-energy value chain. For example, variations across Brazil's states in guidelines and definitions on what can be used in cement kilns underscores the need for national and subnational policies to be sufficiently harmonised in order to enable cement companies to expand co-processing installations across site locations.

Lastly, insights can be drawn from the development of the SNIC roadmap, which has helped to provide clear targets for thermal substitution in cement production in Brazil over the coming decade and beyond. Development of a similar roadmap in Colombia, for instance with Procemco, can help create consensus and a clear vision of how industry can increase capacity for RDF substitutes. The roadmap development process would likewise facilitate and encourage discussions across government and industry stakeholders on the pathways to reduce industry reliance on fossil fuels while identifying the appropriate policy signals and market conditions to enable long-term investment in alternative fuel use.

## Chile: international collaboration for better waste management

In 2015, Chile submitted its Nationally Determined Contribution (NDC)[7] under the Paris Agreement, targeting waste management as a priority sector for the country. Households in Chile generate around 8.1 million tonnes of waste each year, and nearly 60% of that is organic wastes such as fruits, vegetables and garden trimmings (Ministerio del Medio Ambiente, 2020[13]). Only 1% of this waste is recycled, whilst the rest is sent to landfills where it decomposes and releases greenhouse gases (GHGs) such as methane. Overall, Chile's landfills emit more than 4 million metric tonnes of emissions each year, in addition to their wider environmental impact (Arcadis, 2021[14]).

In response, the government embarked on a bilateral co-operation with Environment and Climate Change Canada in 2017 to identify solutions that would accelerate actions to reduce the amount of organic waste going to landfills. The programme, called Reciclo Organicos[8] (organic recycling), aimed to build upon Canada's strong environmental and regulatory expertise in waste management in order to design a sustainable strategy for organic wastes in Chile through four core mandates to support: technology deployment; measurement, reporting and verification (MRV); capital leveraging and co-financing: and community engagement.

One of the major outputs of the programme was the development of a National Organic Waste Strategy (Estrategia Nacional de Residuos Orgánicos, ENRO), which Chile launched in March of 2021 as part of its NDC update. ENRO set an ambitious target to increase municipal waste recovery from 1% to 30% of organic waste by 2030, and to achieve 66% recycling by 2040 (CCAC, 2021[15]). Through recycling and waste management approaches (e.g. composting and biodigestion), the Strategy aims to reduce emissions from organic waste by as much as 70% by 2040.

### *The Reciclos Organicos programme*

Reciclo Organicos was funded under Canada's USD 2.65 billion of climate financing commitment to help countries in their transition to low-carbon, resilient economies (Government of Canada, 2021[16]). The main objectives of the programme was to promote reduction of methane emissions in the waste sector through composting, biodigestion and landfill gas capture.

ImplementaSur, a consulting firm in Chile focused on climate change issues, was engaged to support development of Reciclo Organicos, whose USD 7 million of funding runs from 2017 to 2022. Specifically, the funding supported work with Chile's Ministry of Environment to develop ENRO as well as technical assistance to support municipalities and private sector stakeholders in preparing projects (e.g. supporting site selection, permitting, project engineering and financing). The programme has also co-financed some of these projects, and its support has additionally helped to create a portfolio of waste management initiatives across the country.

One such example is a waste-to-energy (biogas) project owned by biogas company, BioE. The project uses organic waste from a San Pedro vineyard, and BioE installed a pre-treatment facility that can receive different types of waste from farmers and local industry in the region (e.g. salmon farms) to produce electricity and heat cogeneration. The Reciclos Organicos programme supported BioE by providing co-financing for the plant upgrade and with help to pilot blockchain technology for an MRV system. The project is now operational and sells heat to the vineyard, which has a contractual agreement at an agreed price for the heat in exchange for its organic waste. BioE also receives a tipping fee for other wastes received, where the disposal fee charged depends on the type of waste (e.g. lower fees are used for higher energy-content waste). Electricity generated is also sold to grid. In total, the project investment was around USD 5 million for 1 MW of initial generation capacity, which is in the process of being increased to 2 MW.

Another example under the Reciclo Organicos programme is a project under construction undertaken by a landfill in Osorno in the south of Chile. A treatment facility is being built and will be in operation in 2022. This facility will divert organic waste (mainly animal waste from dairy farming and slaughterhouses) from the landfill for use in an anaerobic digester. Development of the project was encouraged in part by calls for circular economy solutions with some of the local companies, who have set goals for zero waste to landfills by 2030. The project will help to capture at least half of the total waste that is currently landfilled, and eventually 100% of that amount could be used for energy production using biodigestion. The producer, Ecoprial, will charge local firms in lieu of tipping fees, where companies were already paying relatively high amounts for treatment of their wastes. Resulting electricity will be sold to the grid, and while there presently is no plan to sell excess heat from the project, this is a future possibility (e.g. to local dairy industries).

Reciclo Organicos also supported Bioenergía Los Pinos[9] in expanding its biogas production and power generation capacity using methane emissions from the Concepción Waste Management Center (Centro de Manejo de Residuos Concepción) in the Biobío region. The project, which is expected to reduce emissions by around 2.3 million tonnes of $CO_2$-equivalent between 2020 and 2040, added biogas cleaning and conditioning systems to existing facilities as well as four new power generation units that increased the previously installed generation capacity from 2.8 MW to 9 MW. Several phases of expansion represented around USD 15 million in total investment (Parra, 2018[17]), where the Reciclo Organicos provided co-financing on the latest expansion, which had a capital expenditures of USD 6.4 million.

In addition, around 20 municipal projects have received support from the Reciclo Organicos programme since 2017. Three will be fully implemented by 2022 (implementation was extended a year due to the COVID-19 pandemic), and the remaining projects will continue to be developed with support from Chile's Ministry of Environment. Programme support depends on the specific needs of each project and can include, for example, identifying the right site, obtaining permits or developing the detailed engineering for the implementation of composting plants. In this process, the Reciclo Organicos programme works with partners, including local governments, to develop first-of-a-kind demonstrations such as composting programmes for this market.

### *An enabling policy environment for market development*

The Reciclo Organicos programme was designed to deliver reductions in methane emissions in Chile, but not explicitly for clean energy development. At the same time, the programme's ambitions required consideration for policy measures and technology solutions that could divert organic matter from landfills, including, notably, ways to leverage private sector engagement for scaled-up implementation.

Waste-to-energy provides attractive solutions to help achieve Chile's emissions reduction ambitions, in addition to opportunities to scale up clean energy investment in the country. To enable those potential solutions, Reciclo Organicos needed to look at wider policy issues to address market development beyond simply managing waste. For instance, a number of policy instruments have previously supported growth of renewable energy technologies in Chile, but incentives have not necessarily been effective for the waste sector (e.g. compared with solar power generation). In fact, as growing solar and wind capacity additions lowered the average cost of electricity production, the business model for waste-to-energy projects became more challenging.

Part of this challenge was the lack of fixed tipping fees for waste. These were set by the market, which previously lacked signals on long-term policy strategies and obligations for waste management. ENRO consequently helped to address this issue by setting clear targets on reduced landfilling, signalling to firms that they needed to find new ways to handle their waste. Decisions naturally depend on a number of corporate considerations, but a critical element of Chile's waste management framework is now a legal policy alternative to sending waste to landfills. The development of regulation on burning methane from landfills, which previously was not clearly recognised, is another critical policy measure under review.

The Reciclo Organicos programme also helped to establish a consistent reporting framework for waste management. Co-operation between the Canadian and Chilean governments included development of an adapted version of protocols for emission reduction accounting and verification in waste management from Québec for the Chilean context. This will help to ensure that the waste sector is properly managed, and digital tools, such as innovative blockchain technology, have been deployed as part of the programme's MRV strategy. In addition to enabling real-time monitoring and recording of emissions reduction from projects (as well as MRV cost savings), these digital tools will allow Chile to show progress on its NDC – a key element for attracting further climate finance.

Monitoring and enforcement for waste tipping is a challenge, but awareness of environmental issues and social monitoring has been growing in Chile. For example, community complaints led to the closure of a meat processing facility that had badly designed wastewater treatment with overflow into the local environment. The resulting closure cost the facility millions of dollars in lost investment. The Reciclo Organicos programme has subsequently worked to build upon this growing public awareness, organising webinars, trainings and other educational events to build a network of stakeholders around waste management. In fact, the programme has nearly 70 thousand followers on Instagram.

Knowledge and capacity building were also a huge part of Reciclo Organicos. Through the process of engaging stakeholders and building consensus on waste management strategies, the programme brought together actors that traditionally did not work together (e.g. banks and municipal authorities). This helped to address Chile's overall policy environment for waste management. For example, composting, previously regulated by landfill regulation, will have a specific set of rules to evaluate its compliance of environmental and health regulations. Stakeholder dialogues also helped to revise action plans under Chile's initial NDC, which was resubmitted with specific mention of organic waste management and the government's intent to tackle this issue moving forward.

### *Lessons learned and implications for the Colombian context*

Collectively, Reciclo Organicos projects are anticipated to save more than 9.8 million tonnes of GHG emissions to 2040 (CCAC, 2021[15]). To date, projects have already leveraged around USD 21 million in capital, highlighting the influence of programme support in creating the enabling conditions for market development. The scale of these investments most likely would not have happened without the focus on waste management and the demonstration of viable business models through the programme's support will help with replication moving forward.

As Colombia seeks to prolong the lifespan of the country's landfills, lessons can be drawn from the Reciclo Organicos programme. Importantly, Chile's long-standing engagement with partners like Canada on environmental issues (e.g. under the Canada-Chile Agreement on Environmental Co-operation[10]) and the government's clear commitment to waste management under its NDC supported the development of the Reciclo Organicos programme. Chile's strategic focus on reducing organic waste to landfilling helped the country to benefit from targeted development co-operation in support of these objectives. The focus also helped to design a more pointed programme (in lieu of a general technical assistance project) to encourage development and replication of solutions that divert waste from landfills, such as anaerobic digestion. This helped to design specific interventions, such as the support for the BioE installation that provided a clearer business model for project implementation, thereby helping to leverage private capital for project development.

The Reciclo Organicos experience also underscores the strategic role of policy to address lack of tipping fees, or low tipping fees, as in Colombia. Improving this critical price signal provides greater incentive for companies to seek waste management solutions, including development of waste-to-energy facilities such as those supported by the programme. Additional signals, such as a carbon credit (e.g. as described under Article 6 of the Paris Agreement) and tax incentives, can further improve the attractiveness of bioenergy solutions. For example, ImplementaSur estimated that the effect of increasing tipping fees by around USD 6 per tonne in Chile would noticeably affect the development of new waste-to-energy projects. Such considerations can similarly be considered in Colombia as additions to the new landfill disposal tax.

Improved enforcement, including through social reporting channels, also supported the underlying business case for development of waste management solutions in Chile. Rising public awareness of the environmental and climate-related impact of landfills has encouraged discussions on waste management and can do so in Colombia, for instance by taking advantage of MME and MADS social networks to create opportunities to monitor waste disposal and discuss alternatives to disposal, such as waste-to-energy projects.

In terms of capacity development, support for knowledge transfer was another important element of the Reciclo Organicos programme. For example, the Los Pinos project benefited from strong connections with a German company, who helped to support technology deployment and local staff development (e.g. working with foreign staff), which helped to bring down costs. These opportunities could similarly be pursued in Colombia and could build upon existing interactive channels such as ProColombia.

Colombia can equally look to expand upon approaches used in the Reciclo Organicos programme to adapt organic waste management solutions and business models to the Colombian context. For example, the household waste collection system in Colombia already uses a fee through electricity and water bills, resulting in a higher collection rate for municipal waste compared to other Latin American countries. An organic waste strategy could take advantage of this billing system to work with local and regional waste authorities to explore development of innovative, pilot programmes that divert waste streams from landfills. These eventual changes to Colombia's successful waste collection services, however, should be carefully balanced in order to avoid unintended consequences such as increased illegal dumping.

Alternatively, financial support (e.g. through blended finance) could be provided on top of current billing structures to encourage innovation solutions and new business models for organic waste management. The Reciclo Organicos programme highlights the role of leveraging financial support to create viable, bankable solutions for investors. Such blended finance solutions (e.g. to enable a pipeline of bankable waste-to-energy projects using standardised documentation) could help to reduce investor risks and increase familiarity with bioenergy developments in Colombia, particularly as commercial banks are still rather unfamiliar with the overall business model of such projects. Development finance and national funds such as FENOGE can thus support de-risking of early market development through financial instruments such as co-financing.

Lastly, a key benefit of the Reciclo Organicos programme has been capacity building to develop knowledge and provide standardised protocols (e.g. MRV using block chain technology) to evaluate projects. This, in turn, helps projects to attract finance and investment. Colombia can look to develop similar protocols for emission reduction in waste management with improved accounting and verification. This can include working with international partners to pilot block chain technology for real-time monitoring and recording of emissions reduction from projects. At the same time, this would support greater enforcement of targets on reduced landfilling, allowing for more assertive signalling to firms that they need to explore alternative pathways for waste.

## Colombia: lessons from cogeneration in the sugar industry

Colombia's sugar crops occupy nearly 197 thousand hectares of plantations, mostly along the Cauca river. Resultant sugar production accounts for 1% of global sugar exports and equally contributes to Colombia being a top global producer of bioethanol through subsequent use of sugarcane bagasse (Asocaña, 2021[18]). The bagasse and other residues from the sugar production process also provide additional co-benefit through electricity and heat cogeneration in the sector. This helps sugarcane producers to reduce their operational costs as well as the need to dispose of waste residues.

Globally, most sugarcane mills have sufficient residues to achieve energy self-sufficiency with remaining capacity for exportable electricity. Existing use of cogeneration in Colombia and elsewhere underscores the financial benefit this waste-to-energy application provides to the sugar industry through revenues from electricity sales, particularly as the sugar industry operates seasonally. These revenues can be supplemented by other financial streams, such as credits from carbon sinks (Zafar, 2020[19]).

### *Use of sugar cane for cogeneration activities: the experience of Manuelita*

Sugarcane cogeneration capacity in Colombia reached 319 MW in 2020, with 134 MW destined for sale as surplus electricity to the gird (Asocaña, 2021[18]). Manuelita, a public limited company (Sociedad Anónima), is one such contributor to these sales and is the third largest producer of sugar in Colombia. It also is the first producer of palm oil and biocombustibles in the country.

Founded in 1864, Manuelita has a long history in sugar production and other agribusinesses, with activities also in Peru, Chile and Brazil. In 2006, the firm began production and commercialisation of bioethanol from sugarcane in Colombia, and three years later expanded this to biodiesel production from palm residues. As these activities developed, Manuelita began using the palm and cane biomass to produce steam and electricity needs at its process plants (Manuelita, 2014[20]).

Manuelita continued to expand its cogeneration capacity using sugarcane bagasse, palm fibre, hulls and rachis, and biogas (biomethane) captured from the liquid waste in the extraction of palm oil. The company began selling surplus electricity to the grid in 2016, notably in support of efforts to mitigate the shortage of energy supply caused by the El Niño phenomenon. In total, Manuelita sold 5 GWh to the grid in 2016, equivalent to the consumption of around 30 thousand Colombian households that year.

Manuelita subsequently expanded its capacity to sell surplus electricity to the grid and by 2018, sales reached over 57 GWh. In order to achieve this, an investment of around USD 18 million (58 billion pesos) was made to install a new turbo-generator at the company's sugar-alcohol mill in Valle del Cauca. The increased sales of surplus power to replace some existing coal-fired power generation, lowering electricity-related carbon emissions by 20 thousand tonnes of $CO_2$ per year in 2018 (Manuelita, 2018[21]).

Outside Colombia, Manuelita also increased investment in power generation capacity at its palm and sugar production facilities. For instance, the company was awarded a 25-year power purchase agreement in Brazil to sell 150 GWh per year to the grid starting in 2021, equivalent to the consumption of 870 thousand households. Investment in the additional generation capacity was at the Vale Do Paraná alcohol mill in Brazil as a joint venture with French firm, Albioma (Manuelita, 2018[21]). In Peru, Manuelita likewise is considering investment in more efficient boilers to be able to sell as much as 28 to 30 GWh per year to the national grid.

In Colombia, Manuelita intends to increase its cogeneration capacity (currently around as much as fourfold by 2024, notably through boiler efficiency improvements. The company already identified 13 plants where such investments would be attractive, where reaching this capacity addition target will require investment of around USD 80 million (equivalent to around USD 2 million for each MW of installed capacity). The cost of investment typically includes connection to the grid (depending on the location), and there are some fiscal benefits as the capacity additions fall under renewable energy incentives. Otherwise, the investment will be paid from revenue from electricity sales, where Manuelita currently sells surplus electricity to a local energy utility at around USD 0.05 (200 Pesos) per kWh. It also sells surplus electricity on spot market, where the price is variable and can be very high in drought periods.

Overall, the return on investment for the capacity upgrades is high, given that with the same feedstock a more efficient boiler can produce even more electricity. Additionally, Colombia's temperate climate and longer sugar seasons mean that residues for cogeneration are available over a considerable period (around 320 days per year), adding to the business case for such investment. By comparison, Brazil, which accounts for around half of global sugar exports, has yields that are 33% less productive than in Colombia (Asocaña, 2021[18]).

In spite of these attractive conditions, one important question remains as to how these capacity upgrades will be financed. Previously, Manuelita has made such investments through corporate finance, but the cost of this debt and the need for upfront equity limit the breadth of total investment Manuelita would normally undertake from such projects. For example, a similar upgrade investment in Brazil was made through a financial partner under a 20-year build-own-operate-transfer model. Yet, this financial structure has been deemed too risky in the Colombian context, in particular due to risk of La Niña events, whose abundant rains reduce the sugar production season. As such, current options for financing Manuelita's expanded capacity are more challenging in Colombia.

### *An enabling policy environment for market development*

Cogeneration in Colombia has grown considerably since early regulations permitting the sale of surplus electricity to the grid were passed under Energy and Gas Regulation Commission (Comisión de Regulación de Energía y Gas, CREG) Resolutions 085 and 086 in 1996. Successive regulatory reforms on grid access rules and the technical conditions for thermal and electricity cogeneration enabled impressive capacity additions in the sugar and palm industries (see Figure 3.1 and the regulatory section above). In particular, early guidelines provided the initial impetus for agroindustry to sell electricity on the spot market, either directly or through a retail agent, drawing interest in the first surplus generation sales, which reached over 100 GWh in 1999 (CCC, 2016[22]).

Still, uncertainty in spot market prices provided little incentive to undertake capital-intensive investments beyond selling surplus from existing capacity. Subsequent reforms in the 2000s increased the business case for making capex investment, but financing of those additions was still a challenge. In particular, regulations regarding cogeneration capacity additions only allowed investment to be taken by the actor carrying out the cogeneration activity. This effectively limited third-party participation, for instance through an energy service business model (UPME, 2015[23]). Moreover, constraints in access to bilateral contracts and limits in accessing the reliability charge auctions meant that the business case for new investments remained weak.

Further regulation in the late 2000s subsequently helped to reinvigorate industry interest, notably through fiscal incentives and clear guidance on access to long-terms contracts. This included important changes in exemptions for payment of contributions on energy destined for self-consumption. For larger firms like Manuelita that could ensure guaranteed power over 20 MW, bilateral contracts also created a clearer opportunity for revenue streams to justify capital improvements. Yet, bilateral contracts through a retailer to supply unregulated customers can be difficult to orchestrate, whilst bilateral agreements directly with a regulator equally depend on retailer incentive. The latter is not facilitated by accounting rules for renewable portfolio standards when electricity is used for self-generation (see regulatory section above).

That said, measures such as CREG Resolution 153 of 2013 on firm energy from fuels of agricultural origin have provided additional incentive for further development of industry cogeneration capacity, notably by improving foresight on revenue streams through long-term contracting. Law 1715 of 2014 equally provided for a number of fiscal incentives (e.g. the 50% income tax reduction) for cogeneration projects and these helped to further improve the economics of capacity upgrades and improvements. The effect of these incentives is evidenced by growth in installed cogeneration capacity connected to the grid.

Overall, changes in the regulatory environment regarding industry cogeneration over the last two decades have increased the underlying business case for actors like Manuelita to continue to invest in capacity improvements and additions. Still, policy reform has not adequately addressed how these projects are financed, where investment through corporate finance may not be a particularly attractive solution for certain companies and may be limiting the amount of capacity additions a firm can take on simultaneously, as is the case for Manuelita.

### *Lessons learned and implications for opportunities moving forward*

The example of strong growth in sugar and palm industry cogeneration highlight the important role effective policy plays in supporting development and expansion of bioenergy technologies. Lessons from experiences in these industries, notably on clear guidance and incentives for industry actors to engage in capacity additions, can be applied to other potential sources of bioenergy, such as biogas opportunities that remain particularly untapped.

The example of Manuelita's experience also highlights some remaining barriers that can be addressed to improve the pipeline of bioenergy capacity additions moving forward. Even in cases where technical and market conditions have been well demonstrated over the last two decades, limitations in the potential vehicles to make such investment may be limiting the speed of new cogeneration additions. Addressing these issues, for instance through regulatory measures to facilitate bilateral agreements with or through retailers, will further help to demonstrate clear revenue streams for development and use of project financing. Financial support, for example through limited revenue guarantees, can equally help to address barriers to project finance for these types of capex improvements. Additional measures such as reforms addressing third-party engagement in these investments will also increase the pool of potential investors in bioenergy cogeneration.

These reforms will also help to increase investment in other bioenergy technologies, such as anaerobic digestion, which remain limited for a number of reasons (see regulatory section above), not least of which is the typical size of such actors, who may not be in the position to undertake direct financing (i.e. on-balance sheet finance) or have access to corporate finance. Investments in these opportunities will require greater access to various forms of finance, from affordable bank loans to co-investment with potential partners and energy service models such as the build-own-operate-transfer scheme used by Manuelita in Brazil. Some of these firms also have limited technical capacity and experience navigating the licencing, permits and connection to the grid. Thus while the existing regulatory framework provides a solid foundation for cogeneration, further policy measures and support mechanisms (e.g. capacity building or a project preparation facility) will help increase the pipeline of self-generation and distributed generation bioenergy technologies.

Additional support for market development can come through improved energy efficiency finance in Colombia. For example, increased cogeneration in the sugar industry can be achieved through investment in more efficient boilers. The return on investment through these improvements is typically high, as it cuts down on operation costs and increases available electricity for sale to the grid without changing the quantity of feedstock. Development of market-based initiatives such as the European De-risking Energy Efficiency Finance Platform[11] and the Investor Confidence Project[12] can help to build investor confidence in these types of energy efficiency upgrades, providing a clear evidence based on asset performance and the return on investment. Such initiatives in Colombia could be undertaken by FENOGE, possibly in collaboration with international partners, to increase affordable financing to bioenergy and other clean energy projects.

## India: foreign investment for paddy straw to biogas in Punjab

Biomass is an important energy source in India, and more than 10 GW of power generation and cogeneration capacity has been installed in the country using bagasse and other biomass sources[13] (MNRE, 2021[24]). India's Ministry of New and Renewable Energy (MNRE) has emphasised the role of bioenergy as part of the country's clean energy targets to 2030 and beyond. Notably, it has highlighted the potential for 230 million metric tonnes of annual agricultural residues (e.g. bagasse, straw, rice and soya husks, coffee waste and cotton stalks) that could be used to produce as much as 28 GW of clean power capacity. An additional 14 GW of bagasse-based cogeneration could also be produced in India's sugar industry.

MNRE has equally supported implementation of biomass capacity development through a number of policy schemes and incentives, such as its national project on biogas development, its New National Biogas and Organic Manure Programme, and its off-grid biogas power generation and thermal energy application programme. These initiatives have supported the development of more than five million small-scale biogas plants (out of an estimated potential for 12.3 million units) as well as the addition of 389 off-grid biogas power projects since 2006. The latter represents nearly 9 MW of off-grid generation capacity (MNRE, 2021[25]). The New National Biogas and Organic Manure Programme also supports refined biogas products such as compressed biogas (CBG), which can be used for other priority sectors like green transport fuels and clean cooking (MNRE, 2021[26]).

### *The Verbio biogas project*

In 2016, Verbio AG, a leading bioenergy manufacturer in Europe, launched the development of new biogas production activities in India. Verbio is a large-scale producer of biodiesel, bioethanol and biomethane, with production plants and bio-refineries globally turning out around 660 thousand tonnes of biodiesel, 260 thousand tonnes of bioethanol and 900 GWh of biomethane in 2020 (Verbio, 2021[27]). The company expanded its activities to India to build upon its experience as an alternative energy supplier in an emerging market that has large, promising bioenergy potential.

Verbio is currently in the process of completing its first biomethane plant in India, which is expected to be operational by the end of 2021. The project, worth around USD 13 million (INR 100 crore) is located in northern India in the Bhutal Kalan village area of the Sangrur District in Punjab. It was approved by the Punjab government in 2018 and is part of a wider agreement for an in-principle approval of nine such future plants in various parts of the state. These are worth as much as USD 120 million (INR 900 crore) in total potential investment (Project Reporter, 2018[28]).

The current plant is being built on a piece of land that Verbio purchased through the normal governmental permitting process. The acquisition and plant development are being financed directly by Verbio through its German headquarters as foreign direct investment. This covers the entire CBG process from raw material supply to biogas generation, transportation and sales. Verbio will purchase paddy straw from local farmers, pre-treat it and turn it into CBG using fermenters built by an Indian company. The CBG will then be transported to filling stations within a 70-100 kilometre distance from the plant for final use in trucks.

Verbio identified India as a new investment market (amongst other countries such as the United States, Canada, Poland and Hungary) given its significant potential for bioenergy development from agricultural, livestock and municipal waste. CBG potential in India is estimated at 32 million metric tonnes of annual output, relative to current production levels of less than 20 thousand metric tonnes (MIIM and EAC, 2020[29]). In addition, agro-production in CBG-relevant sectors (e.g. sugarcane and food grains) has continued to increase since 2015, where Punjab is among high-yield states for biofuel potential.

In this first CBG project, Verbio will convert around 100 thousand tonnes of straw per year to pure biomethane, demonstrating the potential for further capacity growth as well as how bioenergy production can deliver on multiple policy objectives such as reduced fuel imports and job creation in rural areas. Verbio's choice to develop CBG capacity in Punjab was due in part to legislation in India guaranteeing the fuel price at filling stations, while other factors encouraged this first demonstration project. For example, India already has a large fleet of compressed natural gas (CNG) trucks, and density of demand at fuelling stations can reach around 33 tonnes per day for large consumers along key highways. Other CNG vehicles and captive fleets (e.g. taxis) could equally be eventual consumers of CBG, tapping into consistent demand profiles that warrant expanded plant production. There may also be eventual synergies in CBG production, for instance humus (i.e. digestate) from the biomethane production could be burned and used for electricity generation or for heat cogeneration with local industry as secondary markets.

### *Financing biogas development*

While market potential for CBG is promising, this first Punjab biomethane project is not by itself bankable, as it does not yet have guaranteed offtake. Feedstock sourcing, being managed by Verbio, is equally an additional cost to the project, although at the same time, it is necessary to ensure sufficient sourcing of agricultural waste for CBG production. As such, Verbio sees this project as a way to validate the business case for multiplying these types of CBG production units in India, using this first demonstration as a test on the various design elements and potential business model. For instance, the original 2016 plans were looking at bioenergy use for electricity production, but these shifted to CBG production given the low cost of electricity (around USD 0.03-0.04 per kWh) with India's rapidly growing solar and wind markets.

As Verbio looks to expand beyond this initial CBG project, it will need financing to do so. Equity is an option, although this is typically expensive and needs to be combined with debt to lower costs. Achieving expected returns of 10-15% (e.g. compared with other renewable energy developers in India) may equally be challenging for use of equity. In particular, it may be difficult to achieve these rates given current CBG market demand and the need to develop comparable growth in scale (both on the raw material side as well as through procurement/sales) in order to achieve those levels of return on investment. Debt financing could also be used to expand capacity, but interest rates are typically high (e.g. 12%).

India does have available funds for these types of clean energy projects, for instance through MNRE bioenergy support schemes[14] and waste-to-energy financing schemes through the Indian Renewable Energy Development Agency.[15] International finance, for example through KfW, a German state-owned investment and development bank, is also a possible way to expand Verbio's biogas capacity in India. Other support such as de-risking mechanisms (e.g. through a corporate guarantee) would help to address some of these early-market financing challenges.

Policy support can help to address some of these risks, for instance by creating targets or quotas that provide greater offtake assurance. The Government of India is planning legislation to allow some blending in the gas network, and there are also discussions with oil majors, which would help to create sizeable market demand as these companies have around 40 thousand fuelling stations across the country.

Addressing other barriers to expanding biogas production in Punjab and elsewhere in India can facilitate further investment and expansion. For example, recycling humus back to farms will help to maintain source production, and efforts such as capacity building and awareness raising can support this. Farmers have not always seen fertiliser as a good thing, and Verbio has had to work closely with them as part of it sourcing activities, which have an added cost to CBG production. Project development was also relatively long and complicated (it required working with about 50 landowners to acquire land), although Verbio did receive support from the local government, the state minister and the Indian oil minister, which helped in the development of this first project. Notably, Punjab facilitated the Verbio investment through a clear contact point that helped with permitting and approval process, through the Punjab Bureau of Investment Promotion (Invest Punjab),[16] effectively serving as a one-stop shop.

The overall impression from this first CBG project as its development nears completion is that there is considerable room for future growth and investment. Farmers have been happy to be involved, even if they do not receive any money (for now) because it means they do not have to dispose of or burn their waste, the latter having become an important social issue in India due to air pollution from agricultural burning. The government also set targets of 15 million metric tonnes per annum for CBG production by 2025 under its Sustainable Alternative Toward Affordable Transportation scheme[17] announced in late 2018. This will help to drive market demand for CBG as a substitute for CNG with large future growth potential as only around 0.1% of the this target has been achieved to date (MIIM and EAC, 2020[29]). Verbio consequently has plans to build five additional facilities at an estimated investment of around USD 120 million.

### *Lessons learned and implications for the Colombia context*

The Verbio project highlights various market elements and design considerations that influence private sector investment in an emerging clean energy market. Raw material supply, the potential market for the product, local and national legal frameworks (including access to English documentation), and security of investment are all important factors that contribute to investor willingness to step into a new market.

Policy signals such as long-term targets or energy plans, market statistics and energy pricing also help to create an enabling environment for investment. The Verbio project demonstrates how creating these conditions (e.g. in support for accessing/acquiring land for the CBG plant and raw material supply as well as a legal framework and policy environment that signal a market for biogas development) encourage the investor to take on investment risk, even in a nascent bioenergy market. Some of these elements have been addressed and have helped to reduce perceived risks for Verbio, who has taken an investment decision based on future demand potential. By comparison, Verbio found in other countries it considered for potential investment that those essential conditions were still too risky.

As Colombia seeks to increase private investment in biogas, the Verbio case stresses the importance of clear policy signals in supporting developer assessment of risks and returns. Regulations around bioenergy targets and programmes focused on biogas development have helped Verbio to take investment decisions, staking on the government's commitment to executing its biogas strategy. Notably, the Verbio project underscores that future market potential is a key interest in this type of early-stage investment. Such strategic outlooks in Colombia, for instance adding biogas targets for industry and electricity generation, building upon expanded biofuel mandates for transport, would enable similar business ventures.

Other support measures include end-use prices (e.g. for CBG fuel sales) that can increase attractiveness of investment, giving improved investor visibility on potential future returns and encouraging early market development. These price signals also provided an important incentive to develop strategic biogas activities such as work with local farmers in order to capture future needs and opportunities. Colombia could consider similar use of targeted pricing for bioenergy vectors (e.g. biogas) that have notable potential but that currently have limited market use. This would help to drum up investor appetite, whilst equally support deployment of generation capacity that will help improve price competitiveness in the future.

Finally, the case of Verbio illustrates the importance of business facilitation, such as a clear contact point for questions on permitting and approval processes. This can simplify the investment experience for foreign bioenergy developers and investors, who may need support in navigating formal procedures for project development, cutting down related investment costs and time. Support in working with farmers for acquiring raw material input could also help to ensure a clear supply chain, given the fragmented and informal nature of supply in Colombia. This can be done through measures addressing network development, for instance to find potential off-takers like the filling stations and oil companies working with Verbio in India, and will help create a solid business case for future investment.

## Turkey: biogas production from livestock manure

Turkey is an important exporter of agricultural products and ranks as one of the 10 largest agricultural producers in the world (FAO, 2021[30]). Accordingly, the share of the agriculture sector in the Turkey economy accounts for 6.4% of GDP value added (OECD, 2021[31]), and large volumes of subsequent residues with high diversity of agricultural waste mean the sector represents considerable opportunity for bioenergy development. In fact, residues from agriculture are estimated to represent as much as 100 TWh of potential energy. Of this, biogas potential could be as high as 23 TWh, or roughly 7% of the country's electricity generation in 2019 (IEA, 2021[32]). Bioenergy capacity would equally address issues such as emissions and soil degradation from agricultural activities. Livestock in particular accounts for over half of the sector's GHG emissions and contributes to other environment issues from livestock waste (FAO, 2016[33]).

The government's Renewable Energy Action Plan (REAP)[18] set out targets in 2014 to achieve 1 GW of energy from biomass by 2023, compared to 224 MW installed by 2013 (FAO, 2016[33]). This target was surpassed before 2020, with over 1.1 GW of capacity installed by the end of 2019 (Gönül et al., 2021[34]). Bioenergy for power generation alone accounted for 3.2 TWh of renewable electricity in 2019 (or 1.1% of total generation), mainly from biogas. This supported achievement of broader renewable energy targets, achieving 44% of the country's electricity generation from clean energy in 2019, exceeding the goals set in the country's Eleventh Development Plan for 2019-2023 (IEA, 2021[32]).

This impressive growth in bioenergy and renewable energy capacity additions over the last decade was supported by a number of supportive policies. Notably, the Renewable Energy Support Mechanism (Yenilenebilir Enerji Kaynakları Destekleme Mekanizması, YEKDEM)[19] under the Ministry of Energy and Natural Resources (MENR), has offered attractive feed-in-tariffs and other financial incentives for renewable energy projects, encouraging investment in solutions like biogas production across the country.

### *The experience of Energrom Energy in developing biogas capacity*

Energrom Energy is a private engineering and investment company focused on renewable energy, including bioenergy production. The firm was established in 2015 as a partnership between Moots Investment (United States) and the owners of international contracting companies operating in Turkey.

Energrom has three biogas power plants that produce clean electricity and biofertiliser. These include the company's Foça plant in İzmir (3 MW capacity), its Balıkesir plant in Balıkesir (3 MW) and the Kuyucak plant in Aydın (2 MW). All three plants were recently completed in order to benefit from the YEKDEM scheme ending in June 2021. Notably, the projects were finalised under the last round of the scheme as it provided a USD-denominated tariff for a period of ten years.

Energrom also has two further projects under preparation, pending public permits. These will fall under the most recent YEKDEM scheme,[20] valid to December 2025, which offers feed-in-tariffs in Turkish lira, as well as a price adjustment mechanism. Renewable energy investments under the scheme can also benefit from other incentives such as exemptions for value-added tax and custom duties for projects over a given investment size, dependent on the region of installation.[21]

An important element in Energrom's previous and on-going biogas projects has been to secure site locations in sufficient proximity to livestock farms in order to have clear access to residue feedstock. This can be a challenge, as the plants sites themselves cannot be on land destined for agricultural activities. The sites also require pre-feasibility studies co-ordinated with municipal authorities. To expedite this process, Energrom has undertaken the feasibility studies itself and purchased site locations before starting the bioenergy project permitting and licensing procedures. The company also secured supply contracts with regional farmers to have sufficient feedstock for the plants' electricity production, as demonstrating this capacity is required to obtain the plant permits. These supply contracts are incentivised, indirectly, by environmental requirements for farms over a certain threshold (e.g. 500 animals for cattle breeders) to dispose of waste through licenced institutions. Additionally, Energrom provides a fee per tonne of waste, which encourages not only obliged farms but equally those below the regulatory threshold to engage in supply contracts. Some of these supply contracts (e.g. for vegetable and other organic wastes) can also require further environmental permits. As such, the preparatory phases of project development can be relatively onerous and Energrom often contracts a third party to identify and co-ordinate these waste suppliers.

Once its sites are operational, Energrom plant electricity is sold to the interconnected grid on a daily basis through a distribution company, for instance under a fixed tariff through the YEDKEM scheme. Sales can also be done outside the scheme by selling directly through a private distribution company at an agreed price. As long as electricity generators are licensed, they have the right to register in the YEDKEM scheme for any year within the 10-year eligibility period. Generators who negotiate directly with a private distribution company can always register for the YEDKEM scheme the following year.

The choice to sell electricity through the YEDKEM scheme or via a private distributor allows firms to choose agreements with a more advantageous return, which is useful in the case of the Energrom installations, especially as foreign capital from Moots Investment constitutes an important share of finance for the plants. Exchange rate fluctuations already are a potential investment risk, including for capex costs for machinery that is commonly supplied from abroad. Bank credits have been used as mezzanine finance, but to date the projects have not benefited from any concessional or dedicated (e.g. green) lending, as this is still uncommon in Turkey. Energrom is consequently looking into green funds or climate financing opportunities to fund future projects.

Additionally, Energrom has registered its operational facilities under an internationally approved carbon standard, VERRA,[22] which provides carbon emissions reduction certification for the sites such as the 3 MW Foça plant.[23] Turkey does not have a carbon emissions trading scheme in place, and the certification allows Energrom to issue tradable emissions reduction credits on the open market for companies to offset their emissions.

### *An enabling policy environment for bioenergy market development*

Renewable energy sources are prioritised in Turkey's energy agenda under the 2014 REAP. Specifically, the plan set a target for renewable energy to make up at least 30 percent of electricity generation by 2023. This ambition was supported by technology specific targets, including 1 GW of bioenergy, 1 GW of geothermal, 2 GW of hydropower, 5 GW of solar and 20 GW of wind energy (FAO, 2016[33]).

In order to deliver on these targets, the YEKDEM scheme has provided attractive feed-in-tariffs with a local content bonus for generation components manufactured in Turkey. The 2015-20 round of the scheme played an instrumental role in encouraging investment across renewable energy technologies, particularly through USD-denominated tariffs (CIFTCI, 2021[35]). The result was a near tripling of renewable electricity generation in the 2010s (IEA, 2021[32]), and by 2021, investment in renewable power reached nearly USD 66 billion (Erkul, 2021[36]). In 2020 alone, renewable energy financing reach USD 3 billion, supporting nearly 5 GW of new capacity additions (Erkul, 2021[37]).

The new YEKDEM scheme, running to 21 December 2025, will continue to provide a domestic production incentive, with the notable change to feed-in-tariffs in Turkish lira. To address the risks of this denomination for investors, the 2021-25 scheme includes a quarterly escalation mechanism, based on the producer price index, consumer price index, and USD and euro purchase rates. Feed-in-tariffs also were decreased to reflect the declining cost of renewable energy. While the effect of these changes remains to be seen, the added exchange and interest rate volatility risks may be challenging for some projects like geothermal and bioenergy solutions, whose costs have not fallen as significantly as other technologies, like solar and wind. One such example is biomethane feed-in-tariffs, which decreased by 44% under the new scheme, from USD 0.13 per kWh to a 0.54 Lira per kWh (roughly USD 0.075 per kWh in January 2021[24]). This drop does not likely reflect any such cost improvements in new bioenergy generation capacity additions and, as a result, the payback period for Energrom biogas projects, which previous was seven years under the USD-denominated tariff, will likely increase under the new YEKDEM scheme.

In addition to feed-in-tariffs and other economic incentives for renewable energy projects, the Government of Turkey has also taken steps in recent years to simplify clean energy project development. For example, an Energy Investments Co-ordination Board was created in 2016 to facilitate the permitting processes for public and private sector investments in energy projects (Ersin, Arseven and Baydar, 2016[38]). Project developers can also bring investment challenges before the board, which is headed by the vice minister of MENR and is comprised of representatives from various government ministries. The board does not serve as a one-stop shop, for now, and projects are not required to go through the board. For example, Energrom did not use the board and instead pulled from permitting, licensing and project design experiences with other companies that previously had invested in biogas.

Still, co-ordination across the relevant authorities and procedures has helped to simplify and accelerate the investment process (IEA, 2021[32]). For example, the board has helped to inform new regulation that supports renewable investments and particularly investments in bioenergy. It also has helped to increase co-ordination across ministries, which is particularly important for biogas production. For example, use of various animal, vegetable and organic wastes in biogas and biofertiliser production, such as the Energrom facilities, means licensing for these projects can fall under the regulatory frameworks of MENR, the Ministry of Environment, the Ministry of Agriculture and other government authorities. Co-ordination of technical studies, impact assessments, permits, licenses and procedural steps to installation is therefore critical to limiting the time and expenses for project preparation and development activities such as those undertaken by Energrom and its consultancy groups. Once developed, generation licences and YEKDEM incentives have to be approved by the Energy Market Regulatory Authority. Subsequent activities for related fertiliser production (and applicable grants[25]) then go through the Ministry of Agriculture. Thus, the co-ordination helps in ensuring this process is as straightforward and in step as possible. Future measures, such as a one-stop shop for all of these procedures, would further facilitate similar biogas plant development.

### *Lessons learned and implications for the Colombian context*

The Energrom Energy biogas projects will together produce as much as 150 GWh of annual electricity output and around 105 thousand tonnes of fertiliser. This will equally eliminate around 414 thousand tonnes of emissions from the clean electricity output and reduced carbon footprint of agricultural waste, supporting achievement of the government's commitment to increase the share of renewable energy, with added benefits such as improved energy security using locally available energy feedstock.

One important element supporting the development of bioenergy projects such as the Energrom biogas plants is the near-term targets set forth in the REAP strategy to 2023. These provided the foundation for subsequent feed-in-tariffs under the YEKDEM scheme, which alongside other incentives such as tax exemptions have encouraged development of bioenergy and renewable energy additions in Turkey. The effect of recent changes from USD to lira-denominated tariffs will be seen in coming years, though the escalation mechanism should help to address some of those currency exchange risks. The potential impact on bioenergy projects from recent price adjustments also is to be seen, although it underscores an important element in the design of these types of schemes: notably, that use of financial support mechanisms should aim to account for market evolutions to apply public funds as effectively as possible.

As Colombia looks to increase the share of renewable energy technologies in the country's energy mix, including tapping into bioenergy potential, it can clarify short- to medium-term signals under UPME planning in order to reflect policy ambitions in more concrete terms. These specific targets can then be used to assess technology-specific incentives or price signals, such as those under the YEKDEM scheme, to encourage investment in less developed markets (e.g. biomethane production). MME may also want to assess the potential role of other support mechanisms to address eventual risks for bioenergy developers and investors, specifically as the multifaceted nature of these projects (as seen in Energrom's experience) already can have several possible risks through the project cycle (e.g. in impact assessments, licencing, land acquisition and supply contracting).

MME could also consider design of financial mechanisms to address risks for foreign investors. The USD-denominated feed-in-tariffs under the last round of the YEKDEM scheme played a critical role in mobilising foreign capital for Turkey's renewable energy market, supporting phenomenal growth in renewable energy technologies, from 2% of generation capacity in 2010 to more than 15% in 2019 (IEA, 2020[39]). While the risk of a USD denomination was borne by the YEKDEM scheme (and the Turkish government), other de-risking instruments, such as support for a currency hedging mechanism, could be considered to address this risk and attract greater FDI for bioenergy projects in Colombia.

Finally, lessons can be extracted from Turkey's experience with the Energy Investments Co-ordination Board, which is an important step towards simplifying complex permitting and licencing procedures. More recent measures to take this body forward as a one-stop shop will continue to facilitate investment in clean energy development, whilst streamlining processes that can add to the costs and time commitments for project developers. A similar body in Colombia, for instance under MME or the National Planning Department (Departamento Nacional de Planeación), would help to improve institutional co-ordination and address the more complicated nature of bioenergy projects. A one-stop shop, for instance through the ProColombia portal, would likewise facilitate project development and help to attract foreign investment for bioenergy additions, whilst helping to reduce developer time and costs. Additional features could also be added to this portal, for instance targeting bioenergy projects through the platform to facilitate matchmaking between planned and proposed projects with prospective investors.

## References

ABCP (2021), *OECD communication with the Brazilian Portland Cement Association (Associação Brasileira de Cimento Portland, ABCP).* [4]

Arcadis (2021), *Designing a sustainable waste management program in Chile*, Canadian Ministry of Environment and Climate Change and the Chilean Ministry of Climate Change, https://www.arcadis.com/en/projects/north-america/canada/can-chile (accessed on 4 October 2021). [14]

Asocaña (2021), *Annual Report (Informe Annual) 2020-2021*, Colombian Sugarcane Growers Association (Asociación de Cultivadores de Caña de Azúcar, Asocaña), https://www.asocana.org/documentos/1782021-3772D9B2-00FF00,000A000,878787,C3C3C3,FF00FF,2D2D2D,A3C4B5.pdf (accessed on 8 September 2021). [18]

CCAC (2021), *Chile and Canada Partner to Reduce Emissions from the Waste Management Sector*, Climate and Clean Air Coalition (CCAC), https://www.ccacoalition.org/en/news/chile-and-canada-partner-reduce-emissions-waste-management-sector (accessed on 4 October 2021). [15]

CCC (2016), "Cámara de Comercio de Cali", *Cali Chamber of Commerce (Cámara de Comercio de Cali, CCC) Rhythm Cluster (Ritmo Cluster)* 03, https://www.ccc.org.co/inc/uploads/informes-economicos/ritmo-cluster/3.pdf?__cf_chl_captcha_tk__=pmd_InPQWtyNiusgTdfX_gAHa6ciIY8LFy.akEfLyB1rk7w-1632660979-0-gqNtZGzNAyWjcnBszQbl (accessed on 26 September 2021). [22]

Cemnet (2020), *A new destination for waste*, International Cement Review, https://www.cemnet.com/Articles/story/169339/a-new-destination-for-waste.html (accessed on 4 October 2021). [5]

CIFTCI (2021), *Turkey Introduces the New YEKDEM Scheme*, CIFTCI Attorney Partnership, https://www.ciftcilaw.com.tr/content/site-ycap/en/publications/recent-publications/turkey-introduces-the-new-yekdem-scheme/_jcr_content/parsys_article/download/file.res/Client%20Briefing_TURKEY%20INTRODUCES%20THE%20NEW%20YEKDEM%20SCHEME.pdf (accessed on 27 September 2021). [35]

da Silva, R., R. Chaves S. G. Francisco and A. Lopes (2017), "Co-processing of Scrap Tires and Waste from the Re-refining of Used Lube Oil in Cement Kilns", *International Journal of Engineering and Applied Sciences*, Vol. 4/6, https://media.neliti.com/media/publications/257451-co-processing-of-scrap-tires-and-waste-f-c3ca228a.pdf (accessed on 4 October 2021). [6]

Erkul, N. (2021), *Clean power investments in Turkey reach $66B, creating 53% of electricity capacity*, https://www.aa.com.tr/en/energy/renewable/clean-power-investments-in-turkey-reach-66b-creating-53-of-electricity-capacity/33610 (accessed on 5 October 2021). [36]

Erkul, N. (2021), *Turkey's renewable sector to attract $3B fund in 2021*, https://www.aa.com.tr/en/energy/finance/turkeys-renewable-sector-to-attract-3b-fund-in-2021/31845 (accessed on 29 September 2021). [37]

Ersin, B., E. Arseven and C. Baydar (2016), *Energy Investments Tracking And Coordination Board Established In Turkey*, Moroglu Arseven, https://www.mondaq.com/turkey/oil-gas-electricity/475254/energy-investments-tracking-and-coordination-board-established-in-turkey (accessed on 5 October 2021). [38]

FAO (2021), *Turkey at a glance - FAO in Turkey*, Food and Agriculture Organization (FAO) of the United Nations, http://www.fao.org/turkey/fao-in-turkey/turkey-at-a-glance/en/ (accessed on 5 October 2021). [30]

FAO (2016), *BEFS Assessment for Turkey: Sustainable bioenergy options from crop and livestock residues*, Food and Agriculture Organization (FAO) of the United Nations, Rome, https://www.greengrowthknowledge.org/sites/default/files/downloads/resource/FAO_EBRD_Bioenergy%20and%20Food%20Security%20Assessment%20for%20Turkey.pdf (accessed on 27 September 2021). [33]

Gönül, Ö. et al. (2021), "An assessment of wind energy status, incentive mechanisms and market in Turkey", *Engineering Science and Technology, an International Journal*, http://dx.doi.org/10.1016/J.JESTCH.2021.03.016. [34]

Government of Brazil (2021), *R$ 100 million public notice opened for works under the Lixão Zero programme in Minas Gerais (Aberto edital de R$ 100 milhões para obras do programa Lixão Zero em Minas Gerais)*, Government of Brazil, Ministry of Environment (Ministério do Meio Ambiente), https://www.gov.br/mma/pt-br/assuntos/noticias/aberto-edital-de-r-100-milhoes-para-obras-do-programa-lixao-zero-em-minas-gerais (accessed on 4 October 2021). [10]

Government of Canada (2021), *Canada's international climate finance*, Canada's international action, https://www.canada.ca/en/services/environment/weather/climatechange/canada-international-action/climate-finance.html (accessed on 30 September 2021). [16]

Gutberlet, J., T. Bramryd and M. Johansson (2020), "Expansion of the Waste-Based Commodity Frontier: Insights from Sweden and Brazil", *Sustainability*, Vol. 12/7, http://dx.doi.org/10.3390/SU12072628. [9]

IEA (2021), *Tracking Clean Energy Progress: Cement*, International Energy Agency (IEA), https://www.iea.org/reports/cement (accessed on 4 October 2021). [1]

IEA (2021), *Turkey 2021*, IEA, Paris, https://www.iea.org/reports/turkey-2021 (accessed on 27 September 2021). [32]

IEA (2020), *Turkey*, Electricity Information, https://www.iea.org/countries/turkey (accessed on 28 September 2021). [39]

IFC (2017), *Increasing the Use of Alternative Fuels at Cement Plants: International Best Practice*, International Finance Corporation (IFC), Washington, D.C., https://www.ifc.org/wps/wcm/connect/33180042-b8c1-4797-ac82-cd5167689d39/Alternative_Fuels_08+04.pdf?MOD=AJPERES&CVID=lT3Bm3Z (accessed on 4 October 2021). [2]

Lima Cortez, C. and J. Goldemberg (2016), *Cement Technology Roadmap: Alternative Fuels for Cement Sector in Brazil*. [11]

Manuelita (2018), *Manuelita aumenta la generación y venta de energía eléctrica renovable en Colombia | Manuelita*, Manuelita Noticias, https://www.manuelita.com/manuelita-noticias/manuelita-aumenta-la-generacion-y-venta-de-energia-electrica-renovable-en-colombia/ (accessed on 10 September 2021). [21]

Manuelita (2014), *Manuelita completes 150 years producing much more than sugar (Manuelita completa 150 años produciendo mucho más que azúcar)*, https://manuelita.com/manuelita-noticias/manuelita-completa-150-anos-produciendo-mucho-mas-azucar/ (accessed on 4 October 2021). [20]

MIIM and EAC (2020), "India Renewable Energy Opportunities", *Made in India Mittlestand (MIIM) and EAC International Consulting*, https://www.energyforum.in/fileadmin/user_upload/india/media_elements/misc/20200000_Misc/20200430_LR_MIIM_Webinar/PPT_EAC_India_Renewable_Energy_Opportunities.pdf (accessed on 4 October 2021). [29]

Ministerio del Medio Ambiente (2020), *Programa Reciclo Orgánicos: los principales hitos a dos años de su lanzamiento – MMA*, Noticias, https://mma.gob.cl/programa-reciclo-organicos-los-principales-hitos-a-dos-anos-de-su-lanzamiento/ (accessed on 29 September 2021). [13]

MNRE (2021), *Bioenergy - Current Status*, Government of India, Ministry of New and Renewable Energy (MNRE), https://mnre.gov.in/bio-energy/current-status (accessed on 4 October 2021). [25]

MNRE (2021), *New National Biogas and Organic Manure Programme*, Government of India, Ministry of New and Renewable Energy (MNRE), https://biogas.mnre.gov.in/about-the-programmes (accessed on 4 October 2021). [26]

MNRE (2021), *Physical Progress in 2020-21*, Government of India, Ministry of New and Renewable Energy (MNRE), https://mnre.gov.in/the-ministry/physical-progress (accessed on 4 October 2021). [24]

OECD (2021), *OECD Economic Surveys: Turkey 2021*, OECD Publishing, Paris, https://dx.doi.org/10.1787/2cd09ab1-en. [31]

Parra, N. (2018), *Bio Energía Los Pinos de Penco plant expansion approved: it will pass from 2.8 to 9 megawatts (Aprueban ampliación de planta Bio Energía Los Pinos de Penco: pasará de 2,8 a 9 megawatts)*, Biobiochile, https://www.biobiochile.cl/noticias/nacional/region-del-bio-bio/2018/02/20/aprueban-ampliacion-de-planta-bio-energia-los-pinos-de-penco-pasara-de-28-a-9-megawatts.shtml (accessed on 4 October 2021). [17]

Project Reporter (2018), *Verbio to set up RS 100 Crore Bio-gas Plant in Sangrur*, https://projectreporter.co.in/prnews.aspx?nid=5561 (accessed on 4 October 2021). [28]

SNIC (2019), *Cement Technology Roadmap (Roadmap Tecnológico do Cimento)*, National Cement Industry Union (Sindicato Nacional da Indústria do Cimento), Rio de Janeiro, http://snic.org.br/assets/pdf/roadmap/roadmap-tecnologico-do-cimento-brasil.pdf (accessed on 4 October 2021). [3]

Souza, L. (2019), *Brazil generates 79 million tons of solid waste every year*, Agência Brasil, https://agenciabrasil.ebc.com.br/en/geral/noticia/2019-11/brazil-generates-79-million-tons-solid-waste-every-year (accessed on 4 October 2021). [7]

Stewardson, L. (2019), *Cementos Argos increases waste co-processing capacity in Colombia*, World Cement, https://www.worldcement.com/the-americas/10052019/cementos-argos-increases-waste-co-processing-capacity-in-colombia/ (accessed on 4 October 2021). [12]

UPME (2015), *Integration of non-conventional renewable energy in Colombia (Integración de las energías renovables no convencionales en Colombia)*, Planning Unit of the Ministry of Mines and Energy (Unidad de Planeación Minero Energética, UPME), http://www.upme.gov.co/Estudios/2015/Integracion_Energias_Renovables/INTEGRACION_ENERGIAS_RENOVANLES_WEB.pdf (accessed on 16 September 2021). [23]

Verbio (2021), *VERBIO AG - Company Close-Up*, https://www.verbio.de/en/group/company-close-up/ (accessed on 4 October 2021). [27]

Votorantim (2019), *Urban Waste as a Source of Energy for our Plants*, Votorantim Cimentos, http://www.votorantimcimentos.com/en-US/media-center/news/Pages/Urban-Waste-as-a-Source-of-Energy-for-our-Plants.aspx (accessed on 4 October 2021). [8]

Zafar, S. (2020), *Cogeneration of Bagasse*, BioEnergy Consult, https://www.bioenergyconsult.com/cogeneration-of-bagasse/ (accessed on 4 October 2021). [19]

## Notes

[1] For more information, see: https://www.wbcsd.org/Sector-Projects/Cement-Susta nability-Initiative.

[2] For more information, see: http://www.braziliannr.com/brazilian-environmental-legislation/law-no-12305-brazilian-national-policy-solid-waste/.

[3] For more information (in Portuguese), see: https://www.areaseg.com/conama/1999/264-1999.pdf.

[4] For more information (in Portuguese), see: http://www.mp.go.gov.br/portalweb/hp/9/docs/rsulegis_12.pdf.

[5] For more information, see: https://www.in.gov.br/en/web/dou/-/lei-n-14.026-de-15-de-julho-de-2020-267035421.

[6] For more information, see: https://www.in.gov.br/en/web/dou/-/resolucao-conama/mma-n-499-de-6-de-outubro-de-2020-281790575.

[7] For more information (in Spanish): https://www4.unfccc.int/sites/ndcstaging/PublishedDocuments/Chile%20First/Chile%20INDC%20FINAL.pdf.

[8] For more information, see: https://reciclorganicos.com/en/.

[9] For more information (in Spanish), see: http://seia.sea.gob.cl/expediente/ficha/fichaPrincipal.php?modo=ficha&id_expediente=2132658501.

[10] For more information, see: https://www.canada.ca/en/environment-climate-change/corporate/international-affairs/partnerships-countries-regions/latin-america-caribbean/canada-chile-environmental-agreement/overview.html.

[11] For more information, see: https://www.oecd.org/cefim/cross-cutting-analysis/DEEP.htm.

[12] For more information, see: https://www.oecd.org/cefim/cross-cutting-analysis/ICP.htm.

[13] Note : liquid biofuels like biogasoline and biodiesel are also commonly used in India, for example for road transport, and represented more than 875 thousand tonnes of oil equivalent in final energy consumption in 2018 (IEA, 2020).

[14] For more information, see: https://mnre.gov.in/bio-energy/schemes.

[15] For more information, see: https://www.ireda.in/waste-to-energy.

[16] More information, see: https://investpunjab.gov.in/home.

[17] For more information, see: https://mopng.gov.in/en/pdc/investible-projects/alternate-fuels/sustainable-alternative-towards-affordable-transportation.

[18] The National Renewable Energy Action Plan (NREAP), presented under Directive 2009/28/ EC, establishing strategies to promote the development of renewable energy in Turkey.

[19] Published in the Official Gazette in 2011, the Renewable Energy Support Mechanism (Yenilenebilir Enerji Kaynakları Destekleme Mekanizması, YEKDEM), provides feed-in tariffs for renewable power plants, including wind, solar, biomass, hydro and geothermal. Presidential Decree published on 18 September 2020, extended the implementation period for the YEKDEM scheme, by six months until 30 June 2021 due to delays from the COVID-19 pandemic. More information available: https://www.epdk.gov.tr/Detay/Icerik/3-0-0-122/yenilenebilir-enerji-kaynaklari-destekleme-mekanizmasi-yekdem.

[20] Decree No. 3453 published in the Official Gazette No. 31380 on 30 January 2021, outlining the New Renewable Energy Support Mechanism (YEKDEM). This introduces the new feed-in tariff scheme that will apply to renewable energy power plants that become operational between 1 July 2021 and 21 December 2025. More information available: https://www.epdk.gov.tr/Detay/Icerik/3-0-0-122/yenilenebilir-enerji-kaynaklari-destekleme-mekanizmasi-yekdem.

[21] Decision on State Aid in Investments in 2012: hydro, wind, biomass, geothermal and solar all fall under the scope of the general incentive system. Investments must amount to at least TRY 1 million (around USD 172 thousand) in the 1st and 2nd regions, and at least TRY 500 thousand (USD 86 thousand) in the 3rd, 4th, 5th and 6th regions.

[22] VERRA - Verified Carbon Standard. More information at: https://verra.org/.

[23] More information, see: https://registry.verra.org/app/projectDetail/VCS/2347.

[24] Calculated based on the USD-to-TRY exchange rate on 30 January 2021, which was USD/TRY: 7.31.

[25] Declaration No. 2017/22 on the Rural Development Investments Support Program of the Ministry of Food, Agriculture and Livestock.

www.ingramcontent.com/pod-product-compliance
Ingram Content Group UK Ltd.
Pitfield, Milton Keynes, MK11 3LW, UK
UKHW051241300926
15471UKWH00015B/1459

9 789264 804524